Sign of the Dove

Sign of the
Dove

MaryRose's Messages
from the Other Side

MaryRose Occhino

BERKLEY BOOKS, NEW YORK

THE BERKLEY PUBLISHING GROUP
Published by the Penguin Group
Penguin Group (USA) Inc.
375 Hudson Street, New York, New York 10014, USA
Penguin Group (Canada), 90 Eglinton Avenue East, Suite 700, Toronto, Ontario M4P 2Y3, Canada
(a division of Pearson Penguin Canada Inc.)
Penguin Books Ltd., 80 Strand, London WC2R 0RL, England
Penguin Group Ireland, 24 St. Stephen's Green, Dublin 2, Ireland (a division of Penguin Books Ltd.)
Penguin Group (Australia), 250 Camberwell Road, Camberwell, Victoria 3124, Australia
(a division of Pearson Australia Group Pty. Ltd.)
Penguin Books India Pvt. Ltd., 11 Community Centre, Panchsheel Park, New Delhi—110 017, India
Penguin Group (NZ), Cnr. Airborne and Rosedale Roads, Albany, Auckland 1310, New Zealand
(a division of Pearson New Zealand Ltd.)
Penguin Books (South Africa) (Pty.) Ltd., 24 Sturdee Avenue, Rosebank, Johannesburg 2196, South Africa

Penguin Books Ltd., Registered Offices: 80 Strand, London WC2R 0RL, England

This is an original publication of the Berkley Publishing Group.

Copyright © 2006 by MaryRose Occhino
Book design by Kristin del Rosario

First Edition: January 2006

Library of Congress Cataloging-in-Publication Data

Occhino, MaryRose.
  Sign of the dove / MaryRose Occhino.
    p.   cm.
  ISBN 0-425-20544-4
    1. Occhino, MaryRose.   2. Parapsychology.   3. Spiritualism.   I. Title.

BF1283.O27A3   2005
133.9'1'092—dc22
[B]
                                                                    2005047155

PRINTED IN THE UNITED STATES OF AMERICA

10   9   8   7   6   5   4   3   2   1

To my daughter Jackie . . .

It may not be necessary for you to be my legs anymore,
but you're an extension of my heart.
I'm very proud of your journey.

CONTENTS

Acknowledgments

I'd like to take this opportunity to thank my angels, those here in the physical domain as well as those who have made their transition to the Beyond.

I want to pay a special thanks to all those who have helped me throughout the writing of this book, as well as the people who have helped guide me through my life journey. My earth-angels include my children, Chris, Carl, and Jackie; my daughter-in-laws, Angela and Jeannine; my grandchildren, CJ, Danny, Taylor, Tommy, and our littlest princess, Charlotte Rose; as well as my parents and extended family.

I also want to thank Dr. Gary Schwartz. . . . Gary, thank you for listening to your guides and traveling to my home that fateful day in February 2002. You were the first sign that my life would change for the better, and I am forever grateful.

Ray Chambers, the goodwill and positive energy that flow from your being are magnificent, and I thank the Universe for allowing even a minuscule amount to fall my way. Your positive energy is a force to be reckoned with. Dr. Deepak Chopra, thank you for your vote of confidence—just being in your presence was a dream come true. Dr. Christine Dumas, how do I begin to thank you for listening to me while I read my ideas aloud over and over into the wee hours of the morning? The only way I know how is with sisterhood, and that you have. Lynne White, Johanna DeSimone, Nancy and John

Hegyi, and all the rest of my dear friends: Thank you so much for being in my life and making my road so joyful.

To my agents, Johanna Castillo and Jennifer Cayea, thank you for all your hard work and care.

To everyone at Penguin, thank you for believing in my words.

A special thanks to my editor, Denise Silvestro . . . Thank you for holding out (literally) until this book was done. And a sweet and tender kiss to baby Francesca. Thank you for helping your mommy make this book extra special. Your birth is a sign of synchronicity at its best.

Introduction

The Sign of the Dove

One morning, a few months after moving into my home on Long Island, I was awakened for the umpteenth time by the sounds of birds chirping outside my bedroom window. Although annoyed, I thought nothing odd of it. I did, however, call my friend Nancy, whom I had bought the house from, later that day and asked her if she too had had problems sleeping in the morning because of the birds squawking outside. Nancy said the birds had annoyed both her and her husband, John, but they had gotten used to them over the years. I didn't know how I was going to get used to being awakened at the crack of dawn every day. I was at my wits' end. I was already somewhat of an insomniac due to my illness (insomnia is one of the symptoms of multiple sclerosis, a condition I had been diagnosed with six years earlier) and cherished every moment of a sound sleep.

I then asked Nancy why she thought so many birds were in the neighborhood. I mean, this wasn't a couple of birds I was complaining about. It had to be at least twenty or thirty birds screeching outside my bedroom window at the same time. You try sleeping with that going on.

Nancy's response was that she thought there were so many birds because almost everyone in the neighborhood had birdhouses or bird feeders in their backyards. And, she added, she believed there were still a few of them in mine.

Great, I thought. I'll be getting up with the birds every freaking morning.

Like Nancy and John, after a while I got used to the birds chirping. But I was still perplexed as to why one particular bird continued to sound off long after the others had flown away. This bird was different from the others. This bird didn't chirp; it cooed. In fact, it cooed incessantly. This bird, I thought, belonged on Ritalin. He was a hyperactive cooer that didn't shut up.

Because I originally come from Brooklyn, I first suspected the cooing to be the work of the Brooklyn mascot—the pigeon. But I realized I wasn't in Brooklyn anymore. I was some seventy-odd miles from Brooklyn, in what I like to call "God's country." And I couldn't recall for the life of me when I had actually seen a pigeon on my property, or on my block, for that matter. After concentrating on the bird's cooing I realized this wasn't a pigeon at all. No, this bird sounded slightly different from your ordinary, sit-on-top-of-the-building pigeon. This bird's cooing seemed to have class. There was an elegance to its voice that made me rethink my first assumption. Then I saw an image in my mind's eye of what I believed my feathery friend looked like: a graceful white dove. And as a psychic medium who relies on the signs and symbols I receive, I felt confident I finally knew who was making the cooing commotion outside.

Then one morning while lying in bed with the pillow thrown

over my head, a position I had gotten used to sleeping in as I tried to drown out the symphony of the dove, I *snapped*! I couldn't stand another minute of its coo, coo, cooing. It was torturous. "Coo, coo, coo," over and over again. I don't know if it was my imagination, but it seemed to be getting louder and more insistent. My brain felt like it was going to burst if I didn't let out a scream. So I got up from my bed and began yelling at the bird. "Enough already with your cooing! Can you give me a break and shut the heck up?" Never in my wildest dreams did I expect to receive an answer to my frustrated plea, so you can imagine my surprise when the bird responded.

Precisely like the information I receive when connecting with those who have passed over, I began receiving telepathic information from the dove outside my bedroom window. At first I thought it might just be my imagination working overtime. After all, I was a psychic medium, not Dr. Dolittle or the Pet Psychic. I had never communicated with an animal before. Of course, animals that had departed had come through for my clients in their readings. But I had never actually tried to communicate directly with a live animal, and this time was no different. I thought I was just letting off steam at a bird that had made its nest above my bedroom window. But I guess the dove had a few choice words for me too.

The dove telepathically informed me to get up and get ready for a wonderful day. My little buddy wanted me to be excited about all the new and fabulous things that were about to happen in my life. *Confused* is too small a word to describe what I was feeling. Was I hearing correctly? Could this bird actually be giving me a pep talk? And fabulous things were going to happen to me? Yeah, right. Since being diagnosed with MS, *fabulous* wasn't a word I used to describe my life. What was this bird talking about?

At first I tried making sense of it but, foolish me, I had forgotten for a moment the first rule of a psychic reading: never try to make something fit. And the second rule is: logic has nothing to do with life or a reading. That's why it's always better for a psychic to know nothing about her client before a reading. As a psychic I find it easier and more beneficial to the client if I know as little as possible about them. As I always say, it's like painting on a clean canvas.

No, I shouldn't have been trying to figure out why this bird was communicating with me, or what it meant. I should have just accepted it. The bird was just like me—just delivering a message. The bird didn't know about my life, that the possibility of change for me seemed a little far-fetched. The bird didn't know I had a disease and that my days were more or less the same as usual. I gave my readings, all by phone at the time, from my office, a room across from my bedroom. I didn't go out much because of my MS and the exhaustion I felt because of it. So how was my life going to change so extremely, I wondered. Then my little bird-guide interjected a thought into my mind that said, "Watch for the signs of change and then don't hesitate to go forward."

"Watch for the signs of change and don't hesitate to go forward," I repeated to myself.

Although still confused, I mentally agreed to become more aware of any signs of change. And let me tell you, that little bird was right on target, because that very morning the first sign arrived.

A few hours after my message from the dove, I received a call from a woman in California who said she wanted a reading. But this wasn't going to be an ordinary reading. It would be more or less a test. She said if I was as good as Dr. Schwartz had said I was, she was going to try to help introduce me to the public the same way she did for other premier psychics who were now on television. I agreed to the reading and scheduled her for the following day.

Gary E. Schwartz, Ph.D., author of the book *The Afterlife Experiments*, had found me a few months earlier, and I had begun doing scientific research with him and his staff. He was studying the ability to communicate with those on the Other Side. The research with Gary benefited me a great deal. He brought out the natural scientist in me. He made me delve deeper into my psyche and made me start asking myself why I received certain signs, symbols, and messages from those who had crossed over. And I realized that it's not just psychic mediums who receive these signs from the Other Side and from angels and guides. Everyone receives signs, if we pay attention, in the people, places, and things around us. And if we listen closely to the whispers, instincts, intuitions, or whatever you choose to call them, our lives on this plane can change immensely. Notice I said *can* change, not *will* change. Our lives can only change if we allow them to. If we choose to listen, to see, to observe when we're being directed, then anything is possible. If not, all bets are off. No one can make you help yourself; you've got to choose to do it on your own.

So, with the call from this woman in California, my cooing friend had his first validation, and I was going to take heed of what he communicated and not hesitate or be afraid of the change ahead. Her call came out of the blue and I believed it was a sign of a life change, and I was ready. If the bird and I were correct, my reading the following day would go well. And it did. After our reading, the woman from California said that she felt she didn't have to look any further, that in her opinion I had scored the highest of all the psychics she had met. With her help, I started that journey that has taken me to where I am today.

Although my white feathery friend has stopped his cooing—that morning was the first and last time we communicated—I have tried to keep aware of the signs and symbols of coincidence and synchronicity that appear all the time in my life and in the lives of those around me. And what I have concluded is that when we become aware, we are being helped, and if we stay tuned to the signs, signals

and messages being sent, the opportunities for life changes are endless.

I hope this book will help you learn how to decipher the messages
being sent to you all the time. I want you to be able to connect with
your departed loved ones and learn to heed the guides who want to
help you. I also hope that I can show you how to become an earth angel to your friends and family. You don't just get messages for yourself;
there are signs that are meant to benefit others. It is up to us to pay
attention for the good of everyone we encounter. We can be vehicles
of divine intervention, delivering messages from those in the nonphysical world and helping those around us. Open your eyes, open
your mind, and open your heart to receive the signs that can change
lives.

1.

First Step Forward

Deciphering Signs and Symbols

Life is not a journey to the grave with the intention of arriving safely in a pretty and well-preserved body, but rather to skid in sideways, thoroughly used up, totally worn out, and loudly proclaiming . . . Wow . . . What a ride!

—Anonymous

Before you read any further, please stop and take another look at the above quote. If you've done so already, do us both a favor and go back and read it again. Savor it, embrace it, memorize it, and please, please, please, pass it on. Why? Because the contents hold one of the most important lessons you'll ever learn and one of the reasons why I decided to write this book.

Let me clarify that last statement. I thought about writing this book long before I ever had the pleasure of reading the philosophical words above, but the quote itself came to me in such a unique way that I knew it was a sign as to what would help others comprehend what I had been sensing and understanding all my life. The scenario reminds me of the old brainteaser, "Which came first, the chicken or the egg?" Well, I'm happy to say that the answer to the question, "Which came first, my book or the quote?" is a lot easier to answer than the chicken riddle. My book came first, or I should say the reasons I wanted to write this book came to me long before I had ever read the passage.

You see, for more than twenty-five years I have been a psychic medium and my career has led me to the realization that when most people contemplate connecting with the Other Side, they do so because they miss their loved ones enormously and need to be reassured that they're doing okay. But most really don't understand why those on the Other Side want to communicate with us. That's why I decided to write this book, to help you see what the Other Side is trying so desperately to show us.

With each and every reading I've done, I have always informed my clients that their loved ones have jobs to do on the Other Side, and that they don't come through just to say, "Hi, I'm okay! Remember when we went fishing on the lake with Uncle Louie?" That's just not the case. My years of experience have taught me that they send us signs, symbols, and messages because they want us to live our lives to the fullest. They want us to do just what the quote says: go for a ride!

To my surprise, sometimes when I tell clients they're being directed from the Other Side, I get a bittersweet reaction. Some are actually saddened when their loved ones come through with life directions for them. Why? Because they believe the only reason their loved ones would direct them is because they must have regrets about their own lives. That concept, I'm happy to report, is not true. They want to help us, but they are not sad or regretful about their own lives. When they crossed over, they gained insight and now recall their earthly life as a series of valuable lessons. And now they want to share those lessons with us. If you're a parent, how many times have you given your kids advice because you don't want them to make the same mistakes you did? You might have even used that familiar phrase, "If I knew then what I know now . . ." Well, that's exactly what it's like for those who have crossed over. They want to share their new awareness, their new wisdom, with us. If we listen closely, they have answers to many of the questions we ask every day: "Should I leave my job?" "Should I move?" "Where should I move?" And the answer to one of my favorite questions, "How long should I date this guy before I can expect to become engaged?" Of course their responses are different for each and every person that asks, but nevertheless, the answers come. And they give us the answers to these questions and more by simply sending us signs.

Every time I get a sign from my guides, I think about the song by Ace of Base, "The Sign." Don't laugh, but I actually sing the song to myself after I recognize I've been signaled. I've never felt a sad energy when I receive one of these signs. Those who have crossed over have stressed to me that they have jobs to do and whenever their energy comes through regarding their new lives they feel light, relaxed, and happy. I also sense they look forward to advancing their souls and are very excited about their spiritual maturity. And part of their advancement and growth is to help others still here on our plane live the most perfect lives we can.

By now, you may be saying to yourself, "Sure, she's psychic. Getting signs from the Other Side is second nature to her. But me? What kind of signs do I get? Most days I'm so busy running around, working, taking care of the kids, just living life on this side. Who has time to look for signs? And even when I do have quiet time and I hope and pray for a sign, a message—anything—what do I get? Nothing!"

Look, I am a psychic and I've been doing this for over twenty-five years. Recognizing signs *is* a part of my daily routine. But I'm human too, and there are times when my own life interferes with my connection and my objectivity. In times like these I get help through meditation.

Meditation is a very big part of my life, whether I'm perplexed or not. Every morning, before I get out of bed, I meditate for just a few minutes. Nothing extreme, just a few prayers to help me begin my day. But when I know I need extra help in concentrating, I use a different type of meditation. My usual form of meditation is prayer. I generally say the rosary or part of a rosary before I begin each and every reading. This helps me focus and connect to the Other Side. But when I feel the need to connect a little closer or I have specific questions for my guides, I use more of a relaxation meditation to get me to that special place in my head. Not that the rosary doesn't relax me, but a relaxation meditation takes your mind and body to another place and to a different realm. By another place, I mean a place of peace and repose that almost feels like an out-of-body experience. This form of meditation allows you to relax not only your physical body, but also your emotional spirit. It makes you feel light and free from your worries and anxieties, which interfere with your perception. When we're released from the drama and tension of everyday life we're able to calm down our immune system as well as the energy around us. And when the energy around us is peaceful, it makes it much easier for us to receive the messages and signals being sent.

I made myself a meditation tape. When my brain feels wound-up and cluttered and my concentration level isn't what it's supposed to be, I put the tape in my Walkman, flip on my headphones, and sit back. My tape is the result of my years of studying many forms of meditation, as well as direction my guides have given me. I can honestly say that within minutes of listening to it, I'm in a different place. No longer am I concerned with the phone ringing, or worried about how busy my schedule is. My anxieties go by the wayside and by the time the tape is completed, which takes about twenty minutes, I'm ready to connect with the Other Side with my mind wide open and prepared to receive. (Please let me make clear that we can also receive messages when our lives are busy and anxious, but because of the unmanageable energy, we're sometimes not able to hear or see what's being sent as clearly. Being relaxed and at ease makes recognizing signs so much easier.)

If you're having trouble deciphering the signs and messages being sent to you and want to connect and see more clearly, you might want to read through the directions below, then record your own voice on tape, guiding you through the meditation.

Begin by lying down on a couch or bed. Make sure you have on loose-fitting clothing. A jogging suit, or pajamas, works just fine. Nothing should make you feel restrained.

Close your eyes and take a few deep breaths, inhaling and exhaling slowly. Then take a deep, slow breath and hold it for five or six seconds. As you inhale, imagine you are breathing in positive energy and peace. Imagine the air around you is a mist of lavender color and scent, which makes you feel peaceful and calm. With your eyes still closed, imagine the lavender air filling your lungs and working its way through your bloodstream, your muscles, your brain, and your entire being, causing all the tension and outside stimuli to dissipate. Silently count to five then slowly exhale, imagining that you are breathing out all your stress and anxiety. With the exhale, let go of every problem, negative thought, or insecure perception you have of yourself. Continue breathing this way. Every time you breathe in and out, feel your body becoming more and more relaxed and the energy around you becoming more and more serene.

Continue breathing and try to stay focused on your motivation: clarity of mind and spirit. Continue to inhale slowly, hold for five seconds . . . then exhale slowly. Continuously remind yourself that you're breathing in positive energy and peace and breathing out negative energy and anxiety.

Now imagine that the lavender mist becomes a lavender light, glowing all around you. The light gently enters your body from the top of your head, clearing your mind of confusion and healing your body of any physical ailments or discomfort. [I imagine the light dissolving the lesions on my brain caused by MS.] As the purple light enters your body and flows peacefully through your system, your bloodstream, and every molecule of your body, it connects you closer and closer to your higher self, raising your energy frequency so you can connect with ease to your guides and those on the Other Side.

With your mental frequency now beginning to heighten, concentrate on relaxing the muscles of your body. Start by focusing on the muscles in your head and face, relaxing them and bringing a tranquil, soothing, healing energy to them. Continue down toward your neck, shoulders, and back. As you breathe in and out, soothe any aches and pains by calming the energy in these muscles. Continue to soothe the rest of your muscles down to your toes, breathing in and out and envisioning the lavender light healing and tranquilizing your body and washing away all anxieties, all pain, and bringing your entire being to the most peaceful state imaginable.

Next, count down from eight to one. [Why eight and not ten? Eight is my favorite number; it's as simple as that. Use whatever number you want.] As you count down, go deeper and deeper into a state of peace and tranquility, blocking out everything but the sound of your heart beating. . . . Eight, seven, six, five, four, three, two, one. . . . Now imagine that you're standing in front of a white spiral staircase encased in white, feathery clouds. The scent of lavender is now mixed with the smell of newly cut grass, symbolizing spring and renewed life. The staircase beckons you to climb it and you're intuitively aware that once you get to the top you will meet your angels, guides, and others who want to communicate with you and teach you.

Begin to climb . . . and as your foot hits the first steps, a golden light appears and you hear a musical tone, which sounds like a note from a harp. The sound is very peaceful and serene. And as you climb higher and higher, every step your feet touch shines with a golden light and a different note from a harplike instrument is played. You are now in a most blissful state. You have no fear.

Once you reach the top, you walk directly into a large room. There is no door to this room, just a big opening, and inside there are hundreds and hundreds of flowers. There are roses, orchids, daisies, violets, lavenders, tulips, and many, many others. The flowers are all placed in beautiful crystal vases that glimmer from the brilliant white light encompassing the room. You notice that there is furniture in this room—all overstuffed white couches that look like they are made from clouds and cotton candy. The couches are very inviting and you feel as though once you sit on one you'll never want to get up.

Take a deep breath and absorb all the wonderful scents and the energy in the air. The energy in the air can only be described as pure LOVE. You feel loved and cherished. You feel love from the walls, the chairs, and the souls that you intuitively know are present. And most of all, you feel love for yourself. You are happier and more at peace than ever. You are a sponge absorbing all the love a being can possibly hold.

Suddenly, you see someone sitting on one of the couches. As you focus in, you see that it's none other than your loved one who has crossed over. [In my meditation, it is my grandmother Rosie. She smiles and gestures for me to come and sit beside her on one of the white feathery couches. I do so and as we sit and hold each other's hands, another person appears. It's my uncle Hugo; he smiles and kisses me on the cheek and sits on my other side. I know instinctively that they have been guiding me since they have ventured beyond. Once the three of us are sitting together on the couch, the room becomes full of others who I have connected with over the years of my readings and along with them are my guides and guardian angels.] You start telepathically communicating with your loved one (or loved ones) and all the energies in the room, absorbing all the information they are giving you.

You promise you will remember everything they've told you. And just what are they telling you? They are giving you direction for your life and for others who are or will be connected to you. You listen attentively, and before you depart they encircle you and you embrace.

You are aware that your time together is through and it's

time for you to go back to the physical plane. You are not sad or remorseful about leaving and you know they feel the same. You know you can come back at any time and that they will be there.

You get up to leave and are suspended in midair. You are floating and your feet don't touch the ground. Intuitively you know your body is floating because you're inflated with love and positive energy. Your body is reacting somewhat like a balloon inflated with helium. You float to the top of the staircase and as you reach the first step, you are once again grounded. As your foot touches the first step, once again it illuminates with a golden radiance and the harplike sound reappears for an encore. Continue to descend, one step at a time, and when you reach the bottom step, count down from eight to one . . . taking a cleansing breath in between counts. Open your eyes slowly, trying to savor the memory of your journey. You have returned.

Once I finish listening to the tape, my meditation is complete and I am prepared to hear and see whatever signs and/or messages my guides will be conveying. I recommend you try this exercise. You won't be disappointed. The first few times you may find it a little difficult to concentrate, but once you get the hang of it, you'll love the way it makes you feel and you'll also be astonished at how clear the world around you becomes. And if you start paying attention, you will begin to notice signs around you.

In your meditation, ask your loved ones or your guides the questions you want answers to, then become consciously aware of your life and everything around you. Know that your loved ones want to help you, want to give you direction. Then just look, listen, and pay attention. Notice meaningless coincidences. (You know I don't believe there is such a thing as a meaningless coincidence.) Look for signs. It could be a song on the radio whose lyrics speak to you, or an old friend who calls out of the blue. And listen to that little voice inside of you. Call it your gut, call it your instinct, but know that it is guiding you.

I can't emphasize enough that those on the Other Side communicate because they want to help us. And one thing that my guides have shown me time and time again is that we should go after our dreams and live life to the fullest. Let me tell you a little story about something that happened to me a few years ago that illustrates this point perfectly.

It was March 2003, and I had the opportunity to rent an apartment/office in Manhattan. I was confused about whether or not to take it. Actually, confused is probably an understatement. It doesn't begin to describe the fear and anxiety I felt making this decision. My anxieties were not unfounded. I had never driven alone in Manhattan before, and yet I was contemplating commuting over seventy miles, from Long Island to Manhattan, a few times a week . . . with multiple sclerosis no less! What was I thinking? Was I nuts? (I know my daughter might have an opinion about that, but let's not go there.) I really didn't know what to do. Living in the city, even for just part of the time, had always been a dream of mine, but maybe dividing my life and having to commute so far between the two places wasn't the smartest thing for someone in my condition.

I couldn't make a decision, so I started meditating big time. And then, during one of my meditation sessions, my guides gave me a message. They communicated that I just had to ask myself what I should do and I would have the right answer. They had me question how I felt deep down inside the first time I heard the news that the apartment was available. I recalled that day and remembered that I thought two things: it was exciting and it was right. Living in New York City just felt right, and I was excited by the thought of fulfilling my lifelong dream—a dream I had dismissed once I was diagnosed with MS. And my guides showed me that I needed to keep reminding myself that I was no longer a woman stuck within the confines of my home due to an illness. My biggest obstacle now was my fear of change and the fear of being ill.

Of course, this move would be a huge step, and it would be expensive, but it was also something I could and should seriously consider. So I took heed and I listened to my guides and went after my dream. I took the apartment and began commuting, to the astonishment of my family and friends. And I can honestly say that I've never been happier, healthier, busier, and more fulfilled in my entire life.

What my guides have always shown me is that we should go after our dreams so we never have to look back on our lives, once we reach our golden years, and say, "If only I had done that . . ." But please remember, regret only happens on the earthly plane. Once we've crossed over, we do not reflect on our lives here in the physical world with regret or disappointment. I know the concept of our spirit evolving and being happy once we've left this world and having no regrets is really hard to imagine, but that's what I'm told it's like on the Other Side. And by the way, the truth is there really isn't any Other Side (although I will continue to use the term throughout the book for simplicity's sake). It's all this side. So many of us believe that heaven must be some faraway land, but heaven is all around us, both in the physical world and the nonphysical world.

Notice I said nonphysical world and not spiritual world. You know why? Because you don't become a spirit once you've passed over. We're spirits in the here and now. We have souls in the here and now. And it's the same souls we'll have in the afterlife. The only difference is that now we're carrying excess baggage—our bodies. Our lives are infinite because energy is infinite. Once you realize that life is endless, the thought of communication with the "Other Side" or the nonphysical side is easy to comprehend.

Our guides are always sending us signs to direct us. It's up to us to pay attention. We need to trust the messages and our ability to interpret them. Those who have transitioned to the nonphysical world want to lend us a spiritual helping hand, but it's up to us to accept the guidance and take the first step forward. We must remember that they want us to live life to the fullest, take smart chances, and above all, enjoy the journey.

Which brings me back to the quote at the beginning of the chapter. . . .

I knew what I wanted to say in this chapter, but I didn't quite know how to say it. I wanted to explain what signs and symbols were and why they are sent to us. I wanted to share the overriding message that I have been given again and again—to live this life to the fullest. But I didn't know where to begin.

For over a week, I struggled. Of course I had an outline and an idea of how I would structure the chapter, but after I wrote the first few pages and read them back to myself I tore them up. They just didn't seem right. The words weren't flowing with a natural rhythm the way I wanted them to. So, when in doubt, delete, delete, delete, and begin again. But I was optimistic and promised myself I would sit down and find the right words to clarify what I knew in my heart and soul.

Day after day, I sat at my computer attempting to put this chapter together, and I eventually trashed every word I wrote. I needed a clue on how to begin, so I unconsciously asked my guides to help me out with the thought process.

Now, you may be asking yourself, if I unconsciously asked my guides, then how am I aware I asked them in the first place? The answer is simple . . . I was frustrated. And what do most of us do when we're frustrated? We talk to ourselves. Don't deny it; you know you do it too. Even if we don't talk out loud, we all talk to ourselves in our heads, and our thoughts send out messages to the Universe.

Confused? Don't be. I'll explain: our thoughts have the power to change our lives for better or for worse. Please remember what you just read: *for better or for worse*. When you're happy, hopeful, enthusiastic, the atmosphere around you pops with positive energy. You can walk into a room and brighten the day of those around you. And your positive energy can connect with the energies of those in the nonphysical world, creating a pathway for communication.

Similarly, when you are angry, frustrated, or disappointed, the air around you is charged with negativity, and this certainly affects others. Your dark mood can spoil someone's day. If you're annoyed with someone, you'll start becoming annoying to someone else. It's a domino effect. Your negative energy is like a thick, dark cloud casting a shadow over you and blocking you from receiving signs and messages from the Other Side. This effect has been demonstrated time and time again in my seminars. I can't tell you how many times I've noticed someone sitting there with his arms crossed and a scowl on his face. Invariably, this person raises his hand and says something like, "I don't believe in this psychic b.s. I've been to many of these kinds of seminars with my wife and I've never received any kind of message. Can you read something for me?" I'll look at the person, focus, concentrate, and . . . nothing.

The energy is so blocked that nothing can come through. And this person walks away, convinced yet again that there is no such thing as signs or communication from beyond.

But back to my story about writing this chapter. I was really frustrated at not being able to find the right feel for the chapter. I kept writing and rewriting. I was getting ticked off at myself and a little insecure. Could it be, I wondered, that I just couldn't write this chapter? I was agitated, but as I said, I was also optimistic that I would eventually find the right words. I exited my word processor and went directly to my Web site to check my e-mail. I figured I wasn't getting anywhere, so maybe I'd just take my mind off writing for a while and see what happened later.

While perusing my e-mails, I noticed I had loads of junk mail, but there was one e-mail that stood out among the rest. It was from my dear friend Elaine DeLack. I clicked open her note and what did I find but the answer to my silent prayers, the motivation for my first chapter. The wonders of my guides never cease to amaze me. As I read Elaine's e-mail, I sensed my guides standing beside me saying, "Oy, she finally got it!"

Let me backtrack for a minute and explain how the process of my awakening began. Remember that domino effect I mentioned earlier? Well, here we go again. Earlier that day, Elaine had received an e-mail from her friend Bill, and at the bottom of the page was a quote—the quote that opens this chapter—that she felt, for some reason, I would want to read. Let me just clue you in: this was the first time Elaine had ever forwarded me anything from anyone. Elaine DeLack is the inventor of Prokarin, the drug that gave me back my life. Elaine is not a whimsical person. She is extremely analytical and logical and what I believe to be a medical intuitive. She rarely does anything on a whim, and yet she felt this urge to forward me the quote. Why do I think she did it? My guides. My guides are fierce, or so all my friends tell me. For the last few years when I put out a thought or a plea for help, either consciously or subconsciously, I'm answered immediately. I believe my guides gave Elaine what I call a celestial nudge that coaxed her to do something outside her norm, and she forwarded me the passage she had just read. To Elaine it was just a forwarded e-mail, yet to me it was the first step toward the beginning of my book.

Don't think things happen for no reason. Don't dismiss the signs and symbols that are around you every day. Just open your mind and your heart and you will find all the answers you need.

2.

What Are the Odds?

Synchronicity and Coincidence

The intellect has little to do on the road to discovery. There comes a leap in consciousness, call it intuition or what you will, and the solution comes to you and you don't know how or why.
—Albert Einstein

Carl Jung used the word *synchronicity* to describe a meaningful co-incidence or an obvious connection between two apparently nonrelated events. He believed that there was no such thing as a coincidence—that all events are interconnected. Entire books have been written about Jung's theory of synchronicity, and I can't do it justice here, but I do believe he was right. There is no such thing as coincidence. I think "coincidental" happenings are actually communications from the Other Side, nudges from the non-physical world.

When I talk about synchronicity, I don't mean one single event or a single sign. I mean a series of events that, on their own, seem unrelated, but taken together undeniably seem like part of a bigger plan. For example, let's say you're thinking about your dear friend Sue who died last year. As you're reminiscing about good times you shared together, her favorite song comes on the radio. That's a sign. Now let's say you're leaving work and you just miss the bus. It's such a nice evening that you decide to walk home. On the way home, you pass an electronics store and there is a huge sign in the window advertising a sale on stereos. You've been meaning to buy a new stereo ever since the CD player on yours broke last month, but you just never got around to it. You walk into the store and there is an entire wall filled with stereos. Each system is blasting music and each seems tuned to a different station. The noise is deafening, and all the stereos have all these knobs and lights flashing. You're overwhelmed and confused. A salesperson approaches and asks if she can help you. She starts showing you different stereo systems and you notice her nametag says SUE. As she leads you to yet another stereo, you begin to make out a familiar song. You realize that, once again, it's Sue's favorite song. You look at the stereo, you look at the salesgirl named Sue, and you listen to your old friend's favorite song. All of a sudden you know that you've found the perfect stereo. Best of all, there is a one-day special on that particular model and you save a ton of money. Now that's synchronicity!

Synchronicity is not just a quick "hello" from the Other Side. It's like a long telephone conversation, and I believe it is the best validation of life after life that we can receive.

We've all experienced synchronicity. Just think how many times you've said to yourself, "Gee, what are the odds?" after a series of synchronous events happened. As I've said before, it's just a matter of paying attention and remembering that nothing ever happens by chance.

Let me tell you about something that happened to me not too long ago that will show you how synchronicity works. "The Miracle of Arthur Avenue," as I like to call it, happened right around

Mother's Day 2004, and it became a Mother's Day I will never forget.

I was booked solid that entire weekend doing in-house readings at my Manhattan office. In the last few years I had gotten so used to working seven days a week that I had booked myself on Mother's Day without even thinking. That Saturday, my one o'clock appointment arrived right on time. He was a young man in his early thirties who had read my book *Beyond These Four Walls*, and met me in person at a book signing in the Park Slope section of Brooklyn. At the bookstore, he came up to me and requested a private reading. I gave him my card and told him to call my office and I'd be happy to arrange a session with him. That was all we had said to each other, no more and no less. I thanked him for coming and he was on his way. But something about his voice and face made me feel this young man was somewhat special and unique. His energy just felt good.

So now, here he was a few months later, ringing my doorbell. I buzzed him in and waited at my apartment door for him to come up. As I watched him walk up the stairs I got that same sense about him that I had gotten at my book signing: that he was a really good and kind person. I saw a white aura glowing all around him. At that point, I knew we would have a wonderful reading. How could I be so sure his reading would go so well? Because people with white auras are full of positive energy and what I read is energy— your energy and the energy surrounding you. A white aura tells me that the person is centered and on the right life path, and that the energy in their body is flowing without any clogs or blocks, thus making it much easier for a medium to read, and also making it easier for the person with the illuminate aura to receive messages and signs being sent him.

When our energy is clogged or blocked by negativity or just

plain closed-mindedness, our spirit is damaged the same way high cholesterol clogs and damages the arteries to our heart. Just as blocked arteries can cause heart failure, having a clogged natural energy flow can be fatal to your spirit and soul. So if you're one of those health-conscious individuals who watches their diet and checks their cholesterol regularly, do yourself an extra favor and check your energy flow every once in a while. Become consciously aware of how you've been behaving or reacting to specific situations in your life. Check your karma. Question if you could be a better person or more open-minded and more forgiving. And just how do we adjust our karma? Well, it's really quite easy to do. Make a quick mental checklist of what's been happening in your life for the last few weeks. Begin by asking yourself how things have been running at work and at home. Has the energy been hectic or peaceful? If things have been stressful, then it's time to get cracking on finding out the reason why. Is it because of you, or is the stress due to someone else's influence? Remember, you can only fix yourself. All you can do for someone else is to direct them and pass on information that may help them. Next, ask yourself if you feel at peace with yourself and your life. If you can honestly say that there isn't too much you would change, then good for you. That means you're centered and can truly read your own energy. Last, ask yourself how you've been feeling physically lately. Have you been feeling healthy, strong, tired, moody, energetic, or weak? If you've been healthy and energetic, then again I'd say you're in a good place with yourself. If you haven't been feeling like yourself lately and have noticed that you're more tired than usual or more depressed than normal, then think back to what you've been going through lately that may have affected your immune system and then see your doctor for a physical exam.

Always keep in mind that you are your best psychic and that

everything in nature is tied to the natural order of things, the natural energy of life. In other words, everything in our lives affects everything else. So if you start feeling as if your life is running amok, or that there's been just too much drama in your life lately, then go down the mental checklist and keep a psychic eye on your life's rhythm. If you do it often, you'll become much more aware of the natural order of your life and what makes you tick. You'll enjoy your spiritual life as well as your physical life more than ever before once you realize you've always been in charge of yourself. And by checking on your spiritual well-being, you'll be able to clear out bad energy and karma and make your aura glow white.

When I saw this young man's white aura I knew that his energy was positive and that most likely whomever he was hoping to connect with would find a way to connect with me. You see, negativity, anger, viciousness, and resentment block our energy flow and disturb our natural fields of energy. The clearer our energy flow, the easier it is for us to hear and receive signs and messages coming through. So I was looking forward to reading this wonderfully positive individual.

The young man reached the top step and began walking down the hallway toward my apartment. We greeted each other and shook hands. As we did so, I noticed his left hand was holding a tiny white box tied with a red string. He handed it to me and graciously said, "I know from reading your book that you can't eat cookies or sweets, but for some unknown reason yesterday, as I was walking on Arthur Avenue in the Bronx, I had an urge to go in this Italian bakery and buy these cookies for you." Then he added, "Think of them as a small Mother's Day gift for you to give to your family tomorrow."

I thanked my client and put the little box of cookies directly into the refrigerator in the kitchen, and then we walked into the living room and sat at the table and began our session. As I assumed, his reading went extremely well and the hour passed by quickly. He was my last appointment of the day and after he left I relaxed a little by watching television and then went to bed early. Doing readings seven days a week is exhausting and there's not too much time for a social life, but I'm not complaining because this is the life path I chose. In fact, I thank God every day for the honor of communicating with those who have gone beyond and my gift of insight. But before tucking myself in for the night, I looked over my appointment book once more in the hope that somehow my agenda had miraculously changed and I could drive home in the morning to spend the day with my children and mom. But there were no miracles because there, in black and white, staring back at me, were my two appointments scheduled for the next day, Mother's Day. The first one was slotted for 10 A.M., and the second at 2 P.M. With any luck, I thought, I should be in the Midtown Tunnel by 3:20. I was really feeling guilty not being with my kids on Mother's Day, but it was my mistake and my clients had been waiting months for their readings. I couldn't, in good faith, change their appointments. And even if I wanted to reschedule them, there wasn't anywhere to put them; I didn't have any openings until December. So, off to bed I went to be ready for the next day's readings.

The evening news had forecast rain for Mother's Day. I remember smiling when I awoke and saw the sun streaming into my bedroom window the next morning because I had informed a client who had voiced her concerns about the weather not to worry because the news was wrong and the weather, I felt, was going to be just fine with a slight overcast. The sun was my first validation for the day and a good omen for a wonderful Mother's Day, I thought.

My first appointment arrived around 10 A.M. and we were finished in an hour. Just one more reading to go, at 2 P.M., and then I was off to Long Island and my family. When my two o'clock arrived, he kept apologizing for taking up my Mother's Day and I kept telling him not to feel sorry because I believed we were supposed to have a session that day. I told him how I didn't believe in coincidences and how I believed readings were never just one-sided. I explained to him that although he was the one who would be connecting with his loved ones, a lot of the times others, including me, benefit in one way or another from the reading, so it's always a win-win situation.

So, we began his reading and the energy was flowing clearly and his reading, too, I'm happy to report, went very well.

We were finished in a little over an hour and soon I was ready to head on home. I packed my briefcase and overnight bag, locked up my office, and went downstairs to my car, which was parked in front. Just as I put the car key into the ignition I remembered I had forgotten the box of cookies from Arthur Avenue in the refrigerator. "Shoot," I thought to myself. "Do I really want to go all the way back upstairs for a little box of cookies?"

I was getting tired and didn't want to physically tax myself with climbing the stairs again, but something inside my gut kept tugging at me to make the effort, so I did. I schlepped up the stairs, unlocked the door, grabbed the cookies from the fridge, and went back down to the car. I know some of you reading this may think I was just being lazy, and that walking up a flight of stairs isn't such a difficult task. But although I'm on terrific medication for multiple sclerosis, I still get tired and have this fear inside me, especially when I have to drive over seventy miles, that I'll get too tired to drive. But thank God my fears were unfounded and I was fine.

In fact, it was a beautiful drive home. The weather itself felt like a Mother's Day present from Mother Nature. The sun was beaming and I drove home with my windows down and my car radio blaring. It wasn't a bad Mother's Day after all, and I was having a good time singing along to the radio. Funny, though—every once in a while I would find myself staring at the little box of cookies sitting next to me in the passenger seat. I kept thinking, "Who am I going to give you to?"

The first thought that came to mind was that I'd give the cookies to my son Carl when he came by to see me for Mother's Day. After all, he is the family's Cookie Monster. Carl got his nickname not because he ate so many cookies, but because from the first time he ate a cookie as a baby, he would rather eat cookies than anything else. But upon reflection I reconsidered Carl for the Arthur Avenue cookies. "Nah, he's more of an Oreo man," I thought to myself, still glancing over at the box on the seat next to me. "I know, I'll bring them to my parents' house tomorrow!" I realized that I wasn't going to make it to my mother's house today because by the time I got home and unpacked my car I'd be too exhausted to go anywhere. So I gave her a call on my cell phone and wished her a happy Mother's Day and I promised to see her the next day, bright and early.

Still occasionally glancing over at the cookies on the passenger seat, I couldn't believe I was actually excited that I'd figured out the right place for them. Never before have I ever taken so much time trying to decide where a box of cookies should go. But I didn't try to analyze why I was pondering the cookies. I just let it go and drove on home.

The following day I drove to my mother's house, which is approximately fifteen minutes from my home. As I reached the cross-street to her home I looked over and saw a familiar sign. It was a sign I had passed for years, but I had not taken notice of it consciously for more than a decade. The sign was a small billboard outside a chiropractor's office, and it read in black lettering BACK PAIN, NECK PAIN and below that was the doctor's name, Frank Pernice, and his office number. Suddenly a chill ran down my back and up my arms and I knew I was supposed to stop by to see Dr. Pernice. I wasn't sure why, but I had learned long ago to always follow my instincts and this wasn't just a little sign I could dismiss, but an actual billboard. Spontaneously, I turned my car around. As I made a U-turn toward Dr. Pernice's office I found myself looking over at the little box of cookies that I was bringing to my parents' house and it finally hit me. "Arthur Avenue! Dr. Pernice was from Arthur Avenue!" For whatever reason, this little box of cookies had subconsciously suggested I take heed and not just drive by his sign as I had done for some twelve years, but to "see his sign" and pay attention to my senses. I didn't feel that I was supposed to give him the cookies, but I believed the cookies were just a symbol to jog my memory of Dr. Pernice and Arthur Avenue. In hindsight, Dr. Pernice is the only person I know who lived in the Bronx off of Arthur Avenue.

Was this just a coincidental memory jog, or was it divine intervention of some sort? The answer would await me in Dr. Pernice's office. (Since I am not a believer in coincidences, my instincts believed the latter.) The truth is, I don't try to analyze every sign, message, or noncoincidental happening that comes to pass. If I did, I would lose my mind, and so would you because we receive signs and symbols every day, if not two or three times a day. And what I've realized is that if a message or sign is really important for you to decipher, your guides will emphasize its significance by sending you a compilation of synchronous events. So don't worry about missing signs and messages. You'll be contacted. They'll work hard to make you notice them. All you need to do is to be aware they're being sent and become open to receiving them. In the meantime, relax and let your angels and guides do their jobs because they're really good at it.

So, following my sixth sense, I turned my car around and drove directly into Dr. Pernice's driveway. At first I just sat inside my car contemplating what I would say when I saw him. After all, I hadn't seen him in over ten years and here I come knocking at his door out of the blue, saying, "Hey, Frank, remember me, Mary Occhino? How the hell are you?"

Finally, I said what the heck and got out of my car. I walked over to his office door and looked inside the glass window. The lights were out and it looked empty. "He's probably closed," I thought to myself. I decided to leave my business card in the door and write him a short note on the back asking him to give me a call when he got a chance. As I was about to leave my card, his office door opened and there he was standing before me. He looked great, a little more mature than I remembered, but then again I'm sure I did too.

As I stood there in the doorway I felt as though I had been hypnotically regressed into a past life—a life that no longer seemed familiar to me, but that was hidden in the recesses of my memory. The Mary Dr. Pernice had once known no longer existed. No longer was I the person who felt alone and in pain all of the time. No longer was I anxious and fearful of what tomorrow had in store. I had come through the storm and had survived. Hell, I hadn't just survived the storm, I kicked its butt!

Yes, Dr. Pernice and I went back a long way. Back to a time when I didn't have MS, or at least hadn't been officially diagnosed with it. And although Dr. Pernice hadn't been treating me for MS, he had nevertheless been treating me for excruciating back pain due to a herniated disk in my lower lumbar that I had received while working at a job on Long Island. I was a regular patient of his for over a year, sometimes having office visits with him three or four times a week, depending on how I was feeling. Which most of the time was pretty darn bad. I remember the last day I was in his office for a treatment. I was in such bad shape that Dr. Pernice called a neurosurgeon he knew while I lay there on his table. Frank asked the surgeon to see me immediately, and he did. I wound up having emergency back surgery that very day. After my surgery, I spoke to Frank a few times and he had even recommended another physician for me to see when I still complained about excruciating back pain. It seemed my surgery, although somewhat helpful, was unsuccessful, so I started getting injections of Xanacane and cortisone in my spine weekly. Life at that time was not a bowl of cherries and little did I know it was about to take a turn for the worse. About seven months after my first spinal injection, I was hit with my first bout of multiple sclerosis. Like I said, no fruit salads were being made at my house. And after my first MS episode I kind of fell off the face of the earth, or I guess that's the way it may have seemed to Frank.

There were so many times I wanted to call him and tell him what I was going through, but something always seemed to stop me. Now, in hindsight, I'm able to understand that I didn't call him because I didn't want him to feel sorry for me. You see, Frank always went out of his way to be kind and caring to all of his patients and although he was very much my doctor, we had somehow also become friends. Actually, I considered him to be like a younger brother. There was this kinship we felt for each other. I don't know if it was because we were both Italian, but nevertheless, we felt comfortable talking to each other like family. I had seen the shock and despair in my family's eyes when I had told them of my diagnosis and I didn't want to have to see it in his face too.

So, after having had such a close relationship and virtually disappearing, I didn't quite know what to say to Frank when he opened the door some twelve years later.

We looked at each other for a moment, both amazed at all the time that had passed by. The look on Frank's face was that of someone who had just seen a ghost. His eyes were wide and excited, yet not fearful. I guess one could say I was more like a ghost he wished to see. When he finally spoke he asked, "Mary?"

"Yep," I acknowledged, smiling back at him.

"I think about you all the time," he continued, "especially when I have a patient with a bad back like yours was. What happened to you? Where did you go?"

"What happened to me . . . Where did I go, Frank? Well, that's a long story," I answered.

Although his office wasn't open yet, Frank invited me in and we sat in his waiting room trying to play catch-up on each other's lives. I informed him that I had been diagnosed with multiple sclerosis about eight months after my back surgery and that I was sorry I had never let him know. I felt terrible because I didn't want him to think I had dismissed his kindness and friendship, but the first few years I was in total denial, and the fewer people I had to tell the better and the more normal I felt. In hindsight, I realize I was ashamed of being sick. I was embarrassed about becoming disabled. Sound crazy? Not really. What I've learned is that a lot of disabled people feel the same way I did. They feel humiliated about being sick because society as a whole, with conscious and unconscious thoughts, makes you feel different from the rest of the world.

What do I mean by conscious and unconscious thoughts? Think about it. . . .

When you meet someone who has a disability, don't you usually try to be extra kind, or pay a little more attention to them than you would someone who is so-called normal and healthy? Sure, you do. We all do. It's only natural and it's usually not a bad thing to do. That is, unless you're unconsciously thinking when you're looking at the person, "I feel so sorry for you; you'll never have a normal life," or, "Thank God I'm not you." And one of my all-time favorites is the look and/or thought that says, "Oh, my God, now you'll never have another romantic relationship."

Let me just give a little insight to anyone who may have had any of the above thoughts even for a fleeting moment: disabled peole are some of the most psychic people you will ever meet. And they are very aware what you're thinking and how you're feeling, so knock it off! Treat everyone equally. Don't assume that somehow because a person is disabled they are no longer equal to you, because you're 100 percent wrong!

Of course, open a door for a person in a wheelchair. Help a blind person cross the street. Yes, kindness toward another human being is always appreciated. But try to consciously change the way you think about a person with a disability. Remember, some may have a disability, but they are all still very capable of being a human being . . . with the same wants, needs, and dreams as you.

And just another little insight while I'm at it: some people who are disabled or handicapped have some of the best romantic relationships I've ever seen. Some actually have better and longer-lasting relationships than people with unnoticeable disabilities.

What's an unnoticeable disability? An unnoticeable disability is a disability that isn't usually written about in a medical book, nor is it an affliction people are usually given a prescription for.

What I consider to be the most common unnoticeable disabilities are closed-mindedness, insecurity, pride, and being judgmental. Most of those who suffer from any of these "ailments" are very unhappy human beings, yet society still calls them normal. Boy, do I disagree.

Most times I feel that those who are physically challenged in some way are usually gifted in another way. I believe it's the way the Universe evens out the score. Most, I find, are extremely spiritually advanced and their wisdom and compassion are exceedingly acute. They sense things that the so-called healthy people do not. They sense the energy your mind is putting out. So please remember that those who have any sort of medical affliction, as I do, still have hope for their futures and do not need anyone's sympathy. All they need—all we all need—is love, kindness, and compassion, and there should be no label attached to whom you give it to.

Now that I've gotten that off my chest, let's get back to Dr. Pernice and the synchronicity of the Universe.

As I sat in Frank's office and began telling him about all the medical problems I had incurred over the last twelve years, I explained that the reason I wasn't around after my diagnosis was because I was in denial and I really didn't want to have to explain my condition to anyone. You could say that at that time I was inflicted with a little bit of both disabilities, the noticeable and the unnoticeable kind. I say that because I was still healthy enough to be insecure and closed-minded. So I shut myself off from a lot of things and people, Frank being one of them.

As Frank and I spoke and gave each other a synopsis of our lives, I could sense a sadness coming from his energy, but I wasn't quite sure why. You see, it's very hard for a psychic to be objective when she knows a lot about a person. Although Frank and I had a good rapport, I didn't want to just come out and ask, "Why are you so sad?" after not seeing him for so long, but if he were just another client or a person I had just met, I would have asked just that.

So I took the roundabout way and asked him how his wife and children were and he said they were fine. I was happy to hear all was well on the home front, but still I could sense a feeling of loss around him and yet couldn't put my finger on it. Then Frank asked me what I had been up to lately. I told him more about my illness, and I happily mentioned that I had found a medication, called Prokarin, that had taken me out from behind my four walls. I told him that I had bought my own home and had an additional office/apartment in Manhattan.

I could tell he was surprised. "An office and apartment in Manhattan? What are you doing with an office in Manhattan?" he asked.

"I use it to see the clients who come see me in person," I answered.

"Clients? What kind of clients?" Now he was really baffled.

I tried to help Frank recall me telling him, some twelve years earlier in his office, about giving psychic readings and that I had in fact given his receptionist a reading once. He sort of remembered, but he never really gave it much thought, much less considered I would become a professional psychic. And then I realized that we never really talked about it back then because I really wasn't that open about my psychic gifts. There were so many skeptics around, and I was very selective about who I shared my abilities with. Even though Frank was like family, he was still my doctor and most doctors tend to be skeptical, so I was cautious and reserved about my sixth sense.

I also informed Frank that I had written a book (another shock to him), entitled *Beyond These Four Walls: Diary of a Psychic*

Medium, and the office in the city was necessary because it was easier for me to do business there.

"What kind of psychic are you? Are you one of those mediums who talks to the dead?" he asked.

At first I was a little hesitant to answer, because of the usual snickers a psychic receives from those who are skeptical of communicating with the Other Side, but when I looked into his face I knew I wasn't looking into the eyes of a cynic, but into the eyes of someone who was searching for answers. So I answered comfortably, "Yes, Frank, I'm a psychic medium who communicates with the dead."

"Like John Edward and George Anderson?" he asked excitedly.

"So I've been told," I replied.

"How did this happen? When did you realize you could talk to the dead?"

I gave Frank the shortened version of my life, the part he never knew, the intuitive part. I brought him up to date with my business, my book, and also with the research I had done with Gary Schwartz, who wrote *The Afterlife Experiments*.

Frank sat back and took in all the information I was throwing at him. As I spoke I could see the look in his eyes was one of shock and disbelief. But I would soon learn that the disbelief wasn't in me; his disbelief was in the coincidence of my being a psychic medium. You see, my just happening by was an answer to a prayer Frank had recently requested from the Universe.

His mother had passed away unexpectedly in 1998, and Frank had taken it very badly. He just couldn't believe she was actually gone, and since her death he had been on a quest to connect with her and had been trying to get in touch with every top psychic on the East Coast.

"How come I haven't heard about you before now?" he asked.

"Because until recently I never advertised. I was literally locked inside the four walls of my home for almost ten years with MS. Anyone who received a reading from me found me through word of mouth."

I promised Frank that I would drop by the following day with a copy of my book, which would help him understand just what I did and how my career had begun.

In the meantime, I began receiving messages from the energy around Frank, specifically from his mother. She kept showing me a little girl and the number three.

I took the number three to mean three children. I asked Frank if he indeed did have three children and was the youngest a little girl? Earlier, when I had asked him how his wife and kids were, he never mentioned how many children he had and I just assumed he only had the two boys I had known about prior to us losing touch.

Frank acknowledged he did have three children and the youngest was indeed a girl. "How did you know?" he asked. I told him I assumed so because his mother was making me see and feel certain things about his children. She kept showing me the number three and I saw an image of a young girl. And for some reason she made me stay stuck mentally on my image of a little girl. I asked Frank if his mother had been here when his daughter was born. He said no, that she had passed when his wife was seven months pregnant with their daughter. "My mother," he said, "never found out the baby was a little girl."

"Ah, but she does know, Frank," I said. "That's why it's so important for her to come through with this information." I explained that when a person leaves our physical plane and they connect with us, they are not just coming through with messages or validation from our memory of them. More important, they are coming through to tell us they are still aware of what's going on in and around our lives, and that they are still a part of them.

Frank was dumbstruck. He couldn't believe this was happening to him.

It wasn't that Frank couldn't believe he was getting a reading; he was stunned because he had recently gotten so exhausted searching for a sign from his mother that he had surrendered his requests to the Universe because that was all there was left to do. He said he had told his mom that if she was around and was trying to reach him, he was here waiting. And when we truly surrender and let go of our anxieties, we receive our answers much faster than we could have ever anticipated.

Here are six steps to surrendering that you may find helpful:

1 ♦ *Let go of anxiety.* Stop worrying about what's going to happen tomorrow. Live in the present.

2 ♦ *Have complete faith.* Know in your heart that the outcome will be a positive one. (You'll receive your answers.)

3 ♦ *Set no timetables.* Never give yourself a timetable for things to happen. When we don't, things happen much faster than we ever anticipated.

4 ♦ *Give up by never giving up.* Surrender only your old habits and preconceived notions about life. But be determined that you'll do everything possible to allow your desires to come true. Give up and let go of anything negative (people included) surrounding your hopes and desires.

5 ♦ *Persevere against all odds.* Remember that nothing is too great or too big for you to accomplish—nothing! Even though there

will be people around you who think you're just a dreamer, stick with your instincts.

6 ◆ *Keep it in your heart.* Don't obsess about your desires. Try not to even consciously think about them. Just keep them in your heart and keep yourself open to the possibilities.

Frank had truly accomplished the art of surrendering because when he finally stopped searching and let go of his anxieties about connecting with his mom, his wishes and desires came true. His mother, in turn, went through enormous efforts to make sure a message got through to her son. Frank's mother sent him a Mother's Day gift of synchronous events which began their manifestation at a book signing in Brooklyn, continued with a box of cookies from Arthur Avenue in the Bronx, and finally concluded at her son's office door on Long Island.

Were they all just meaningless coincidences?

Think about it. . . . What are the odds?

3.

Finding Your Way

The Art of Surrendering

One of the most difficult—but definitely the most beneficial—lessons I have learned is the need to let go and allow the Universe to take care of things. If you're a type A personality like me and have a hard time relinquishing control to anything or anyone, relax in knowing you're in good hands when you allow the Universe to take the wheel every now and then. The "now and then" times are the times when you've done all you can do to make something happen, but you're at a standstill and nothing is happening fast enough or the way you had planned. In fact, you may feel you're getting nowhere fast or as though you're running backward instead of forward. At times like that, try thinking of the Universe as the largest, most powerful, most indemnified insurance broker in the cosmos. That's what I do when I need to let go of my anxieties. I sometimes mentally replay that popular insurance company slogan we've all grown up hearing—"You're in good hands with . . ." Well, instead of quoting the popular insurance company's slogan, I think: "You're in good hands with the Universe."

Can you think of anything or anyone who has more clout or know-how than the Universe? I can't.

The Universe can cover every need we have or ever anticipate having. The Universe can literally cover all our life bases. Not just what an ordinary insurance company would handle, like our homes, cars, health, or physical lives. The Universe can cover our spiritual lives as well. *The Universe can indemnify our souls*. It can and will lead us in the right directions, always. The Universe *never* makes a mistake. Never! We're the only ones who can screw up our lives when we don't go in the direction the Universe is sending us, especially when we're supposed to be surrendering and we're not.

I know you may be thinking, "Sure, surrender sounds good on paper, but it's easier said than done." Well, my friend, I understand your uncertainty, if that's how you feel, but please believe me, surrendering and letting go of my fears wasn't easy for me by a long shot either. But if I didn't surrender, my fears would have owned me, and I'm too independent for that. In fact, from the time I was a little girl, I was independent and went after what I wanted. I wasn't the shy, quiet, sugar-and-spice type of youngster who waited patiently for things to come my way. Maybe it was the Brooklyn in me, but I had a fiery spirit and a determined will. I remember when I was in the eighth grade, the last year of elementary school. I had been attending the same school since kindergarten and was looking forward to graduating with the classmates I had known since childhood. But then the Universe kind of sideswiped me and turned my whole world upside down all in one day, or so I felt at the time. Thinking about that day even now, some forty years later, still makes my heart ache.

It was September 1965 and we had just returned to school after summer vacation. We were back no more than a week when one night after dinner, my mother and father sat my brother and me down to discuss something they said was very important. Charles, older than me by exactly four years (we were born on the same day four years apart), would graduate that year from high school and we were both excited about the parties we would have for our mutual graduations. But our excitement bubbles were about to burst in one fell swoop. Or, should I say, with two words: "We're moving!"

I remember Charles and me looking at them like they had both lost their minds. We couldn't be moving, we thought. Our parents had lived in this apartment their entire married life, which at the time was twenty-five years. And my father had lived in the same apartment with his parents and sister before he was married to my mother. So they had to be joking, because there was no way we were going to move, now or ever. Our apartment was a part of us. We were 588 Union Street.

"What do you mean we're moving?" Charles and I cried out in unison.

"We have to move," my father said. "The landlord sold the house, and anyway, the neighborhood is just getting too bad."

Everyone knew that the Red Hook section of Brooklyn, our neighborhood, was tough and kind of worn out, but we loved it. We were used to it and we coped. But my parents had other ideas. They made up their minds and that was that. They continued and said that not only were we moving, but we would also be moved out by October 30!

"Where are we moving?" I cried.

"Bensonhurst," replied my mother. "Near Grandma."

"No way!" Charles and I both yelled. "We're not coming!"

My brother and I both threatened to run away from home if we moved, but my parents weren't buying any of our threats. They had one consolation for my brother, and that was that he would be able to continue going to his high school because he was old enough to ride the trains alone. But I would have to change schools because they couldn't allow me to take a train and bus in the morning and evening the way Charles was going to have to, because I was just too young.

I thought I would die.

My whole life flew in front of my eyes. My heart was broken. I knew no other life, and now I wouldn't even be graduating with the kids I had known since birth. I would no longer be with my best friends Debbie, Frances, and Connie. "This can't be happening," I thought. "Why is God doing this to me? Why?" I asked my mother.

"God's not doing anything to you; we're just moving because we have to," she replied.

I stood silent for a moment and thought. I remember thinking I had to find a way to get to graduate with my class and not fight with my parents. Not because I was a saintly child, mind you, but because I wasn't going to win if I fought with them. I had learned early on that when my parents made up their minds, that was it. I had to find a loophole, and I did. My argument was that Charles went to school on Sixth Avenue, not too far from my grammar school. My school was only three avenues down and a few blocks over from his. So why couldn't I commute with Charles every day?

My brother wasn't buying it. His first reaction was that no way was he going to ride the train every day with his baby sister. But he must have seen the look of despair in my eyes and took pity on me, because a few minutes later he was helping me present my case to them. They finally agreed that since he had to be at school around the same time as me, it wasn't out of the question for me to take the train with him in the morning. But—and here came the hard part—coming home from school would be the problem. Charles had track and basketball after school and wouldn't be able to commute home with me, but my parents didn't want me to take the train all by myself. So I came up with another solution . . . I would take two buses. (My parents felt more comfortable with buses because they were out in the open, with more people around for safety.) I would walk from Third Avenue to Fifth Avenue and Union Street then ride the sixty-some-odd blocks to the Sixtieth Street bus. Then I'd take that bus up to Sixteenth Avenue and walk the four blocks from the bus stop to our new apartment. To me it sounded so easy, but to my parents it was a nightmare.

I remember my mother saying, "Do you know how hard that's going to be once it gets cold out? And you know, in the winter it gets dark early. That's much too much for any kid to do."

But I wanted to graduate with my classmates and my friends more than anything. Even if it meant I had to get up every morning at 6 A.M. and get home every night at 5 P.M. How many kids do you know today that are willing to commute four hours a day just to go to school? But my parents agreed and my brother promised that when he didn't have practice or a game he would travel by train with me. And my father sometimes drove us to school in the morning—sometimes. Most times he had to be at work by 5 A.M.

So I guess you can say I learned how to surrender at a very early age. Now remember what I said about surrendering. We surrender *only after* we've done everything we can to make happen what we want to have happen. The Universe taught me early on that when we take care of ourselves, it will watch out for us. And I finally found out why the Universe taught me that very tough lesson: it was getting me ready for the rest of my life.

Even as an adult, I always believed in taking care of myself. That's why when I was diagnosed with an illness that can make you dependent on others, I couldn't bear it. In fact, the one thing I actually hate is being dependent on anyone. Don't get me wrong—we all need someone in our lives, and we really never do anything alone. Even if you take a bus, someone has to drive the bus to get you where you want to go. But for me, having to rely on someone to do my everyday chores was like a living hell.

So, being diagnosed with MS was a big blow not only to my physical body but to my state of mind. Now not only did I have a chronic illness, but also one that weakened me so much that I was forced to become dependent on others for the first time in my life. MS had not only weakened my muscles but also had weakened my immune system so much that I became extremely sensitive to literally everything around me: foods, perfumes, medicines, cookies, pasta . . . everything. With each attack I became weaker and more sensitive to something else. And when the attacks were over (which sometimes took six weeks or six months), I would always find that there was something else I could no longer do. First it was cooking. Or at least the way I was used to cooking. I couldn't take the heat in the kitchen from the stove or oven. So the five-course meals most Italian mothers cook for Sunday dinner was gone.

The next thing to worsen was my walking. Sometimes I was left with a limp from the numbness on the side of my body where the attack had taken place, which also left my legs weaker and weaker as time went on.

Then there was the shopping, then the driving. Finally, when I could no longer drive my young daughter to the supermarket to shop for us, I had to call a shopping service. How I hated that! I remember seeing the look in some of the other shoppers' eyes; if you have, or have had, such an illness you know what I'm talking about. The look that says, "You poor thing, you're so sick and so doomed." Even if they weren't really thinking I was doomed, their looks made me feel that way. I know some of you may be saying, "Hey, I wish I had someone to shop for me. I just don't have the time." Well, that's a different thing altogether, because if you call a shopper to shop for you because you just don't have the time, it's your choice . . . big difference. To someone like me, who had been independent since I was a child, who was married and out of her parents' house at the mere age of seventeen and a mother at eighteen, having to ask someone to help me because I had no choice was the worst aspect of the disease. But I realized that the doomed feeling that I had been sensing was only bringing me down further into the darkness of the disease, and in order to be lifted out of the gloom and into the light I had to surrender.

I had to do everything in my power to try to get myself better and I had to trust that the Universe would take care of me, the same way it had taken care of me when I was a kid traveling the two hours every morning to school.

These days, people might still consider me strong-willed, always taking the bull by the horns—after all, you can take the girl out of Brooklyn, but you can't take the Brooklyn out of the girl! But I have learned the hard way that if I let go of my anxiety and trust in the Universe, I will be taken care of, and so will you.

Speaking of taking the girl out of Brooklyn . . . 1989 was right about the time I was to get reacquainted with the mighty lesson of the art of surrendering and get a not-so-subtle reminder that the Universe knows exactly what it's doing.

In 1987, my daughter's father, Dennis, and I had separated and I moved from Long Island to Bensonhurst, Brooklyn, with my children. It wasn't easy, for me or for my kids. We went from living in a nine-room home on Long Island, with a manicured lawn and a built-in Grecian-type pool, to a small four-room apartment in a six-family house in Brooklyn.

Our lives were turned topsy-turvy for a while, but I thought I was adjusting pretty well to being a single parent yet again, and the kids seemed to be doing fine too. God bless them, kids are really resilient. Although their lives were uprooted, they very rarely complained and actually seemed to be enjoying themselves. All in all, I'd say they were doing a lot better than me. The boys quickly made friends, and Jacqueline loved that Brooklyn had sidewalks. She would ride her tiny bike all day long, back and forth, on the weekends, when I was home from work. With the help of my high-school friend Claire, I found a job at an insurance brokerage company in Manhattan. I found day care for my daughter, and the boys were in high school and doing well. We all settled into a comfortable routine and life seemed to be moving along fine. Sure, at times it was hectic, but I did what I had to do: work, pay the bills, and take care of my kids.

Looking back on it now, I realize I was always under a lot of pressure to make the rent, get food on the table, and make sure my children were happy and well adjusted. I really didn't feel the stress building up, but I guess it was, because about a year later, in 1989, everything started to hit the fan. The stress I had put upon myself and had been ignoring started to weaken my immune system, and that's when the rest of the dominoes began to fall.

In May of that year, I was hospitalized for the first time. I had kidney stones that led to a massive kidney infection called pyelonephritis, and that kept me in the hospital and on intravenous antibiotics for almost two weeks. Just a few months after that, in August, I was hospitalized for three weeks and put into traction for a herniated disk. And then, believe it or not, about six weeks later in October, I was hospitalized yet again to undergo a hysterectomy. It was crazy! I kept asking myself what I had done so wrong in life to deserve all this bad karma. I hadn't cheated in my relationships. I didn't take advantage of or bully anyone. And although I was sure I was far from perfect, I tried to be a good person. So what the heck was going on with me, I wondered, to make my health deteriorate so rapidly?

I eventually figured out that my physical state was declining because the energy surrounding me, inside and out, was much too nervous and dramatic. I was ready to explode from the pressure I was under. I guess I did explode internally, and it affected my health, my organs, and my nervous system.

I rarely relaxed and was always on the go, never allowing my nervous system to rest. I was always worried about money and was obsessed with being the best mother I could be. I was upset most of the time, thinking maybe I had done the wrong thing by moving to Brooklyn and leaving Long Island. And while I slept—or should I say, while I didn't sleep—I tossed and turned, playing this mental tug-of-war, asking myself the same questions every single night for about a year: "Did you make the right decision in leaving?" And "Couldn't you have just been satisfied having a pretty good relationship?" I knew I was suffering from insomnia because I felt guilty about taking my children from such beautiful and lush surroundings to a cramped apartment in Brooklyn. I had taken my daughter from her father and her home and had to cart her to day care at 6:30 every morning. And what about my boys, did I do the right thing by them? Was their Brooklyn school as good as the one they'd attended in Long Island? All through the night I would toss and turn, but when morning came, even though I was exhausted, I had to put aside my doubts and anxiety and do what I had to do.

But while I was doing all I had to do and not sleeping, and just generally being a nervous wreck all the time, I never allowed the energy around me to relax. I never gave myself a chance to chill out and take in positive energy. Or replenish my depleted energy. Think about it . . . even your car needs gas when it's empty. Well, your body and spirit are your vehicle. You have to maintain it in order to run well both spiritually and physically. In fact, the spiritual and physical parts of us work hand in hand. If one is lacking something, then you can bet the other is too.

How do we replenish our depleted energy? The first answer that comes to mind is to be around happy and positive people. Remember energy is contagious, just like an airborne virus. It's in the air and we breathe it in, even if we can't see it. So being around happy, positive, gregarious people would be the first step toward an energy fill-up.

My second suggestion would be to meditate to relax your mind and body. Then take a nice warm bath and a short nap. Taking time to *not* think about your problems, while you relax your muscles in warm water, is like taking a mini-vacation—and it's a lot less expensive! Light scented candles in the bathroom to add that extra energy boost. Lavender-scented ones are my all-time favorite, not just because I like the aroma but because of how relaxed I feel when they're lit.

Back then, I was just a little grasshopper learning my lessons the hard way and just trying to do the right thing, but you know what? I know that I did the right thing. I couldn't have stayed in my marriage. It wasn't that my relationship was abusive, but it was empty. I wanted a marriage in which I and my partner truly cherished and adored each other. I had made myself a promise, some would say a contract with the Universe, after my first failed marriage that if I couldn't have the complete emotional package of love, honor, and respect I would go it alone. I had to follow through on my promise. I now view what I went through as a means to learn the lessons I needed to learn.

That doesn't mean every lesson we learn has to be painful, and every promise we make to ourselves must have a high price. It means that if you believe wholeheartedly in your convictions and you make a verbal contract with yourself and put the information out there into the Universe, you have to follow through. Be true to yourself and don't look back. Trust your first instincts and have faith in your decisions. It's easy for me to say this now, but I've learned that you can't second-guess yourself, because when you do, that's when keeping your promises becomes painful. That's exactly what I was doing to myself every night back then. I would question my decisions to separate from my husband and move to Brooklyn, and I built up a lot of anxiety and stress. And it was this stress and anxiety that affected the energy that surrounded me and made me sick.

Unfortunately, my declining health wasn't the only negative consequence of the toxic energy around me. Just when I was ready to go back to work after my hysterectomy, I was laid off from my job. They told me they were downsizing and my position was being eliminated. I'm sure their decision was influenced by the substantial amount of time I had to take off from work due to illness, but in any event it was another domino falling—an additional problem in a chain reaction of negative energy.

I was upset about losing my job—after all, I had a family to support. But what could I do? If they no longer wanted me, I would just have to find another position. I could handle it, I thought. After all, I managed to deal with my health problems, and if I could handle those I could handle anything, right?

Wrong! Remember the old saying, "When it rains, it pours"? Well, the forecast around me was for monsoon rains, and it was coming down in buckets! A week after I got laid off, my landlord knocked on my door and told me that he had sold the building and the new owners wanted my apartment for themselves. I had sixty days to look for a new place to live.

At that point in my life, calmness was *not* one of my attributes . . . and to be totally honest, it's still not one of mine now. I have to work on surrendering my aggravation and anxiety every single day of my life in order to maintain the quality of health I've become accustomed to. And let me also add that the rain still comes down every now and then, but not in full buckets. The rain nowadays feels more like someone shooting me with one of my grandson's water guns. Water guns, as we know, can be lots of fun on a hot summer's day, but after a while even a good thing becomes annoying if it's sprayed in your face persistently. And in hindsight, in 1989 I felt as if I were in the midst of a tsunami with nowhere to run. My energy was exhausted and my physical well-being was at stake. I felt as though there was no time to recoup from my last battle with the Universe before I had to try to figure out my next move.

I tried looking for another apartment in Brooklyn, but nothing that suited us was available. The job situation was looking dimmer and dimmer as the days went by. I went on countless interviews but didn't get any offers. I had an impressive résumé, but I kept coming up empty. I'm sure it was because I was completely honest with all the prospective employers and disclosed that I had been sick for a while and then lost my job. I guess I could have kept my mouth shut about my private medical history, but I'm an absolute believer in karma, and I knew that if I wasn't completely honest, it would only cause something else negative to happen to me down the road. I also believe that when we are honest and do the right thing, we develop a good and positive karmic path and everything somehow works out for the best. But, as for jobs in the Big Apple . . . I was coming up with worms.

I can laugh about it now, but back then I was ready to pull my hair out of my head. If I ever felt squeezed by the Universe to go and do something else, this was the time. So I did what any redblooded Italian American woman would do in my circumstances . . . I called my mother.

After four weeks of looking for a new job and a new apartment, in desperation I called my parents on Long Island and asked if my children and I could live at their house for a short time. My mother was happy that we'd be moving back to Long Island; she said that of course she would make room for us, just as she had done some twelve years prior when I had separated from my boys' father. But, I told her, there was one difference now: I did not intend to stay for a long period of time. I was on a mission to find a job and a house to rent as soon as possible. My children needed stability and security. Although my moving back into my parents' home may have seemed like history repeating itself, this time around I was much more mature and had grown mentally as well as spiritually and intuitively. I knew that I was finally in charge of my life, and I knew what I had to do. I began to seriously visualize the future I wanted for my children and myself.

I mentally voiced my intentions to the Universe as I said my prayers and asked for help in finding a job. I explained to God, and whoever else was listening, that the job I received didn't have to be a management position, or even an administrative one. I was willing to do anything I had to do to support my family—within reason, of course—to get us back on our feet.

I thought about my father. He was a longshoreman most of his life, but when the ILA—the International Longshoreman's Association—would go on strike, he would work as a fruit peddler to support his family. He would get in his paneled truck, go down to the fruit market, and fill it up. Sometimes the back of the truck was filled with just watermelons, sometimes with just bananas, and other times with a mixture of every kind of fruit that was in season. And on special occasions, or just because the weather was nice and he wanted some company while he drove around the neighborhood, my father would bring my brother Charles and me along with him for the ride. Boy, how we loved those times.

My father would shout in a singsong voice from his truck as he double-parked in front of the buildings: "Bananas! Watermelons!" Sometimes I would yell melodically right along with him. I remember the people looking out their windows, searching for where the little voice was coming from and then waving and smiling down at me. We usually didn't venture out of our own neighborhood, and most of my father's customers had known him for years. They would hurry down to the truck and buy whatever fruit my father was selling that day. My father told me the people always got a kick out of me, but he never coaxed me to say a word. If I felt like yelling along with him, I did. In fact, the first time I echoed his cry, it was more of a shock to him than to anyone else.

Those days in the fruit truck are perhaps some of the best memories I have of my childhood. I loved spending time with my father, and I learned such valuable lessons. Those times taught me to never worry about not having a job. If money got tight, I could just fill up my truck and go sell fruit. Not literally of course! But it taught me that sometimes we have to think outside the box, look beyond what we may think is the right or only job for us. When the longshoremen went on strike, my father didn't wait around looking for the perfect job. He sold fruit. He taught me I should never think a job not worthy of me, because you make the difference in a job. You can make the meekest job into a golden opportunity. He also told me to always remember that when one door closes, you open the next door—don't wait for someone to open it for you. He taught me to go out there and do it myself!

But perhaps the best lesson I learned from my father is that if a child doesn't feel that their parent is capable of running their own life, how confident are they going to be about you running theirs? My father made me feel secure knowing he would always come through for the family. We didn't have to worry because as long as he could breathe, he would have a job.

I wanted my children to feel that same kind of security. I wanted them to know that I would do whatever it took to make this happen. And if that meant moving back in with my parents and taking whatever job the Universe placed before me, then by God, that's what I'd do.

So the three of us—my son Carl, my daughter Jacqueline, and myself—moved back to Long Island in July 1990. My son Christopher stayed behind in Brooklyn with his father and prepared to begin college that fall in upstate New York.

Our adjustment to Long Island and to my parents' house went well, but after two weeks, I still hadn't found affordable housing or a job. Then one day, out of the blue, a family friend dropped by the house. His mother, whose name was also MaryRose and who was also known to be very psychic, had recently passed away. He mentioned that instead of selling MaryRose's house, which was now unoccupied, the family had decided to put it up for rent. He asked if we knew anyone suitable who would be willing to rent it.

When I heard those words—"House for rent!"—come out of his mouth, there was absolutely no doubt in my mind that his mother had somehow heard my pleas and was responding to my appeal. The reason I was so sure was that as soon as our friend mentioned his mother, the first thought that popped into my head was that this was supposed to be: MaryRose wanted another MaryRose to live in her house. This thought was immediately followed by the theme song from the old Mighty Mouse cartoon: "Here I come to save the day . . ." I knew MaryRose was sending this message to me. Sounds crazy to you? Well, try living in my head.

The house was perfect for us. It had plenty of room, it was in my price range, and it was just down the road from my parents' house. That was an added bonus, because one of my dilemmas was trying to find a house in the same school district as my parents' home because the school bus would have to pick up my daughter from there and drop her off in the afternoon, and the only way I would be able to make that arrangement was if I lived in the same school district and told them that my mother was the babysitter.

This house being available for rent was far too wonderful to be just a coincidence. To me, it was a miraculous twist of fate and a sign that our lives were changing for the better. It was a sign, I believed, that I was finally on the right track and I would be able to replenish and gas up my positive energy. You don't have to be a psychic to know that we took the house. And the first day we moved in, we received a magnificent welcome sign that the house really was meant for us.

My brother Michael and my son Carl were helping me move. When they finished bringing in all our furniture from the moving van, I asked them if they could help me move the refrigerator because I wanted to wash the floor back there. It was something I learned from my grandmother, who believed that before you go to sleep the first night in a new home or apartment, you should always make sure you wash all the floors, vacuum all the rugs, and clean all the windows. She also told everyone to make sure we bought a new bottle of cooking oil, a box of salt, and a new broom. And before we washed the floor, we should sprinkle some salt on the floor and sweep it out the door to get rid of the prior energy in the house. This was an old Italian ritual passed down through the generations.

Michael and Carl moved the refrigerator and I began to sweep and mop the area. As I was about to pick up all the dust and grime that was on the floor, I found a magnet that must have fallen behind the refrigerator years earlier. It was so full of grunge that it couldn't have fallen anytime recently. For some reason, instead of just throwing it into the garbage, I decided to wipe it off and see what words were hidden beneath the dirt. I took a little household cleaner and sprayed it directly on the magnet. As I wiped it clean, I began to see what was hidden under all that grime, and my eyes filled with tears. Without a doubt, this little magnet was a message from beyond that I was in the right place at the right time. I sprayed some more cleanser so I could get the magnet completely clean and placed it on the refrigerator.

"Hey, guys, come look what I found," I called to Michael and Carl.

As they neared the refrigerator, they said in unison, "Holy [you know what]!" They were surprised and amused when they saw that the magnet read MARYROSE'S KITCHEN.

What are the odds of me moving into the home of a woman who was also an intuitive and had the same name as me? Talk about your signs! And as far as I was concerned, this little magnet's significance couldn't have been any greater if it was a billboard in Times Square. I felt more positive than ever about our move, and I finished the cleaning of the house the way my grandmother had taught me to, with happy anticipation of our new life on Long Island.

Now all that was left to do was find a job. I went on daily job interviews, but the jobs I was offered didn't pay enough to cover my rent and other household bills. Then, just when I was at the end of my rope, my mother called me and told me to come over to her house because my uncle Richie, her baby brother, was over for a visit and wanted to talk to me.

My uncle Richie and I had always been close and I considered him more like a big brother than an uncle, since he was only eight years older than me. Looking forward to seeing him, I immediately hopped into my car with my daughter in tow and drove up the road to my mother's house. When I got there we hugged, glad to see one another. I couldn't remember just how long it had been since I had seen him last. We made small talk for a few minutes and I updated him on all that had been happening in my life, and what wasn't happening as far as me getting a job. Hesitating for a moment while he thought, my uncle asked, "Mary, how would you like to work with me in the meat department as a meat wrapper?"

My uncle remembered that when I was a teenager I had had a part-time job as a meat wrapper in a supermarket, so he knew I was familiar with what the job entailed. It was far from an easy job and the meat department was always cold, about forty-five degrees, but the pay was good and so were the benefits.

My uncle also knew it was a far cry from the jobs I had had in the past. But it was a decent job and had great insurance benefits for the kids and me, and the salary was higher than any of the offers I had been receiving of late. So I took the job and a few days later began working side by side with my uncle, who trained me for a few weeks until I got the knack of how things were done with his company. Talk about your culture shocks! I was used to going for lunch at a restaurant overlooking Rockefeller Center; now here I was sitting on milk crate eating pizza in my white butcher's coat (which was sometimes covered in animal blood). But, the meat department was my paneled truck and I was willing and able to fill it with fruit to support my family. And I quickly got my sea legs, or in this case I should say my chicken legs, and fit right in. The Universe had heard my intentions and, as usual, come through.

Sometimes life doesn't go the way we plan. So many of us make elaborate plans—meticulous timelines for when we'll marry, have children, where we'll live, what we'll be. And then something comes along and throws a monkey wrench into the works. We get divorced, we lose our jobs, we have fertility problems, etc. Our carefully laid-out life takes a major detour, and we bang our heads and struggle to get back on track. It will drive you crazy. You'll feel like you've lost control. But what I want you to remember is that sometimes what seems like a detour is actually the Universe putting you on the path you're *supposed* to be on. How do I know? Because it has happened to me. Do you think two failed marriages, moving back and forth between Brooklyn and Long Island and finally to Manhattan, getting MS, working jobs that ranged from radio traffic manager to meat packer to professional writer, psychic medium, and now radio host was part of my plan? Sure, I'm psychic, but not even I could have predicted this crazy life! But you know what? In my heart I know that I'm exactly where I'm supposed to be right now, and every single thing—good and bad—that has happened in my life has led me here. It's the same for you. We just have to surrender ourselves and trust that the Universe knows exactly where to lead us. And if we pay attention, there will be signs along the way, like road markers, that will let us know we're heading in the right direction.

4.

Room 217

Trusting the Universe

As I mentioned earlier, in today's society, everywhere we turn someone is telling us, via television, radio, lecture, or books, how we can or should strive for perfection in our careers, families, and just about every other aspect of our lives. So it's easy to see why, as we're soaking in all this good and constructive information, trying to stay one step ahead of the next guy, many of us have become obsessed with finding our true life path with the hope of creating our most perfect universe. A universe of self-empowerment. I believe one of the most commonly used phrases in the long list of self-improvement literature today is something like *How to find the power within us*. And you know what? I don't disagree. In fact, I agree 100 percent with it. I concur that we all need to learn that we have the skills and the power within us that will guide us toward our dreams. In fact, I hope this book will help teach you how to do just that.

But while we're striving for perfection in the idyllic world we've mapped out for ourselves and learning how to become the most perfect multitasking employee, the kindest, sweetest, richest mommy and daddy—or, in my case, grandparent—while we're trying to accomplish social perfection, we've got to trust that the dreams we dare to dream can actually come true.

So get the party started right now by telling yourself that you'll allow the Universe to teach you how to swim in the ocean of life. Consciously surrender your hopes and fears to the Universe and trust that it will hear you and not let you get pulled down by the undertow. Permit yourself to fall freely into the Universe's arms and trust that the Universe will help you take care of yourself! And keep in mind that it doesn't matter what you have or haven't gone through already in life; we all need to learn how to give up our power in order to become stronger.

We all have different needs and wants, as well as hurts and fears. Some of us may have already felt despair and grief because of the loss of loved ones; others may have felt hopelessness due to illnesses or tragedies in their lives; last but far from least, others may have felt desolation and rejection because of romantic situations or career issues like losing their jobs. Everyone has and will have their own cross to bear, as mothers like to say. And everyone has their own journey in life. But always keep in mind that we never walk, cry, laugh, or think by ourselves . . . someone or something is always watching us and guiding us. We always have company . . . we have the Universe.

If and when those trying times come in your life, that's the time for you to give it up, to surrender and trust in God, or what some of us are more comfortable saying, trust in the Universe. But whatever you choose to call or believe the higher power *is*, by all means please believe there *is* a higher power. Because something much more powerful, much greater than us mere humans is taking care of us and making sure things in our world are happening as they should.

I know that while you're experiencing your own private pain it's sometimes hard to believe anyone could observe the anguish you're going through and not do anything about it. But they are . . . you are being helped, even though you may not feel like you are and you're not aware of it. All you have to do to sense that help is to believe and trust in your intuition. Believe in what your gut is telling you, no matter what anyone else may say the outcome is supposed to be. Believe that there is a reason for what you are going through, a plan beyond what you can recognize at the moment. Even if the day comes when you're the only one believing in you . . . *keep believing in the outcome you have planned for yourself.* Believe beyond a shadow of a doubt in your passions and trust that the Universe is there for you and will always be there for you. Believe in the signs and feelings you receive, and your life will be a much happier place.

When I first told people that I believed I would get better after being diagnosed with MS, I didn't have to be a psychic to know that more than one of them thought I was delusional. More than one doctor told me that I should just face the facts and come to terms with my diagnosis and my future. They told me I had a disease there was no cure for, and that my condition would only get worse with time. Of course, there was a possibility that I could go into remission for a long time, but, by the way my disease seemed to be progressing, it didn't look likely. You know what I was thinking the whole time they were speaking to me? "*Baloney!* . . . You don't know me and you don't know what I believe my outcome will be!" I knew the whole time that, by hook or by crook, somehow, some-way, someday, I would be better.

So to all your naysayers, you have my permission to quote me. Tell them all, *Baloney!*

Never allow society, or even your own insecurities, to discourage your beliefs or your instincts—never! Whether you have a yearning for a specific career, something that you've had a passion for forever and you feel that you are meant to do, or you feel strongly about any other thing in your life—don't give up or give in. Believe that the Universe is allowing you to feel what you're feeling because it's right.

I remember one time when my trusting in the Universe literally became a matter of life and death. . . .

After my meat-wrapping indoctrination with my uncle in Rocky Point, I transferred to the meat department of a supermarket in Riverhead for a few months. It was hard work but the pay was good, and I was grateful for the opportunity to support myself and my children. After a while I didn't mind the cold and I got used to the noise of all the machinery. In fact, as I stood in front of the meat-wrapping machine, I would often let myself be soothed by the rhythmic cha-cling as another tray of chops or sirloin would be fed into the metal monster and sealed in plastic. But not that day. That day, my mind was full of thoughts of my father, who was undergoing surgery for an inflamed prostate. I wanted to go to the hospital with him, but the doctors told us it was a simple procedure, that he wouldn't even have to stay in the hospital overnight. My parents insisted I go to work since the job was still relatively new. But still I was anxious.

I thought about the conversation I had had with my father the night before. I had gone over to my parents' house after work, as I usually did, to pick up my daughter Jacqueline, who my mother babysat while I was working. When I got there my father called to me to come sit with him a while he rested. This was my first clue that something wasn't right. My father never napped or rested. Even though he had had a stroke some twenty years earlier, he was always vibrant and full of energy. So why was he in bed so early?

I sat in a chair next to my father's bed and he started talking about his surgery. We went over all the reasons why he had to have the operation the following day, but I could tell he didn't have a good feeling about it. This was the first time in my life I had ever heard a hint of fear or apprehension coming from him and it worried me senseless. My father had a great sense of humor and a sarcastic wit and was usually very positive about any kind of medical course of action. But there was something in the sound of his voice that night that struck me as strange. Was my father's fear a sign that something was going to go wrong? I tried not to read into the situation, because I had learned that when I'm too involved with an issue or a person, I sometimes can't see objectively. So I did the only thing I could: I comforted my father by saying that I was sure everything was going to be okay, that the procedure was minor and he was going to be in good hands. As I said those words I silently prayed that my prediction was correct.

I didn't remember my father being as vulnerable as he seemed that night. This was a new experience for me and I was slightly shaken by it because my father was usually the one who reassured everyone else in his rough-and-tough style. This time I had to be the tough one. I told him that he was still as strong as a bull and that he could pull through anything. I also told him what his choices were, which weren't many: he could either have the surgery tomorrow or remain with a bag attached to his bladder for the rest of his life—an option I knew he didn't even want to consider.

After I had said all I could to alleviate some of his fears, I went home. But as I drove the few blocks to my house, I was filled with guilt because I honestly wasn't sure that I believed everything I'd told my father.

I prayed myself to sleep that night, asking my angels and my father's angels to keep an eye on him as his doctors performed their medical task, and I prayed again as soon as I opened my eyes in the morning. Before I went to work I called my parents' home and asked my mother how they were holding up. She said they were both a little nervous, but doing fine, and that they were going to leave for the hospital in a few minutes. I asked to speak with my father for a quick second. I tried to reassure him again. I told him that he'd be fine and that I'd see him when he got home that evening. And before I hung up, I told him that I loved him. Shyly, my father said he loved me too. With all that said, I hung up the phone, got into my car, and drove my daughter to her father's house, so he could babysit her for the day. Then I drove the twenty miles to work, all the way with a knot in my stomach, anxiously worried about my father. At 8 A.M. I arrived in Riverhead, my head full of thoughts about my father. There I was, trying to calm myself with the repetitive sounds of the meat-wrapping machine.

My anxious thoughts were interrupted by the sound of the supermarket loudspeaker: "Phone call for the meat department, please pick up."

I knew in my heart that the call was for me. I had been feeling particularly anxious in the few moments before the announcement and I felt a terrible pain in my stomach. I said a silent prayer for my father and waited to hear who the phone call was for.

One of the butchers picked up the phone and said, "Meat department. Mary? Sure, she's here. Hold on."

Even though I was expecting that the call was for me, hearing the confirmation was like getting punched in the stomach. I was so nervous I thought I would vomit, and I wasn't sure if my legs would carry me to the phone on the other end of the room. I knew this was the call that would say my father was in trouble. Something had gone wrong with the operation. I was hoping I was wrong, but something just didn't feel right. I remember saying to the Man up above, "If I am right, dear God, let him still be alive."

From the moment the phone rang until I picked it up, I felt as though everything were moving in slow motion. But once my hand touched the receiver everything went back into real time. I grabbed the phone, took a deep breath, and instead of saying hello I asked, "Who's this?"

"Ma?" the familiar voice of my son Christopher asked.

Chris had come up for a few weeks to visit with us before he had to head off to college. He was at home when my mother called from the hospital.

"Ma, Grandma just called. Grandpa's not doing so good."

"What's wrong?" I cried. "What happened?"

"There were some complications with the surgery and Grandpa had another stroke," he said, now choking on his tears.

Chris told me to get to the hospital as soon as I could. My father was unconscious since his surgery and was in ICU.

Feeling faint, I hung up the phone, threw off my white coat, and announced as I ran to the exit, "It's my father. He's in a coma. I've got to go."

I got into my little Omni, which my father had recently given me to go back and forth to work. He was no longer capable of driving and it was just sitting in his driveway anyway, so he figured he'd put it to good use by giving it to me, and I was extremely grateful. I dashed out of the parking lot and drove as though the Omni were a Corvette Stingray, racing on the Long Island Expressway to St.

Charles Hospital in Port Jefferson doing about eighty. (I do not recommend anyone driving the way I did. I know it's no excuse, but I was in a state of shock and I really shouldn't have been driving in the first place.) I made it to the hospital in less than fifteen minutes, parked the car, and ran to the admissions desk to ask where ICU was. They told me to go to the second floor and I raced to the elevator. Once again, everything seemed to be moving at a snail's pace. The elevator felt like it took forever to go up one flight. I could have run up the freaking stairs faster. When the elevator door finally opened, I saw about fifteen people from my extended family. I looked around for my mother or my brothers, but they were nowhere in sight. Finally, in the corner of the room at the end of the hall, I spotted my brother Charles sitting with my cousin Leo, both looking very sullen. I ran over to Charles and asked him, "What the hell happened to Daddy?" My brother Charles then clued me in to what had actually occurred.

It seems that before the surgery began, my father told the surgeon that he had decided that he didn't want to be put under. He wanted a local anesthesia so that he would be up and could hear and see what was going on. The doctor did not recommend he have that type of anesthesia because he felt my father would be more relaxed if he was fully under. But my father insisted that he wanted to be awake in case he had to talk to the doctors or nurses. His doctor, realizing that my father wasn't about to change his mind, agreed to his wishes. They used an epidural and talked to my father through each step of the procedure. What they had to do was open a path to his inflamed prostate, what my father jokingly described as roto-rootering his plumbing. And as they went into his bladder with their instruments my father began to feel terrible pains in his stomach. He told the doctors what he was feeling and said to them, "Whatever you are doing to me is hurting me. You've done something wrong; I'm having pain all over now." Ironically, it was because my father was awake that he was able to alert the doctor immediately that something was wrong.

When the nurse checked the monitors, she saw that my father's potassium level had dropped dramatically and informed the doctor what was going on. My father, in the meantime, kept telling the doctor to stop what he was doing because he was feeling immense pressure and pain, so the doctor stopped. But the next time they checked my father's vital signs, they saw that his blood pressure had risen extremely high and that almost all the potassium was depleted from his body. He wound up having a stroke right there on the operating table, and now, more than three hours later, he still hadn't regained consciousness.

I wanted to scream. I had promised my father just the night before that he would be okay and had advised him that the surgery was necessary. And it was necessary; we all knew he had no other choice, because my father had stated time and time again how much he hated having the bag attached to his bladder. But still I felt guilty. I felt like I had lied to him.

I just wanted to see my father now. Charles pointed toward the room he was in and I walked over and entered. My mother and brother Michael were in the room with him. They were both red-eyed and pale, and I heard them talking to my father, trying to wake him out of his sleep.

I began to walk toward my family when the nurse on duty stopped me and said that only two visitors were allowed at a time in the room. Hearing this, Michael volunteered to leave so I could spend some time with my father and mother.

My father looked peaceful and seemed to be resting. He wasn't hooked to any machines and was breathing on his own. He did, however, have an oxygen tube connected to his nose. Other than that he was snoring away.

I looked at my mother, who looked like she had aged ten years since last night, and said, "Don't worry, Mom, he'll pull through." I then asked the nurse who was standing by about his prognosis. She said that only time would tell and that it was a good sign that he was breathing on his own. As she said that, I started noticing that my father's breathing and snoring seemed different somehow. I asked my mother if she noticed anything and she said she didn't. I then went outside the room and asked my brother Michael to come back in for a minute because I wanted his opinion on something.

"Michael, does Daddy's breathing sound different to you?" I asked.

Michael listened for a moment and said, "No, he sounds the same. He's snoring away."

I told my mother and brother that I thought they were both wrong. Something in the rhythm of my father's breathing had changed and I wondered why they didn't notice it. I shared my concerns with the nurse and suggested that maybe my father needed to be hooked up to a ventilator. She listened for a moment, restated that my father was breathing on his own, and said the same thing my mother and brother told me . . . that I was wrong.

By this time, I was becoming infuriated and told the nurse that I wanted to see a doctor immediately. Instead of calling a doctor, she asked me to leave the room and said it was understandable that I was distressed, but my father was in "good hands" and that she knew what she was doing.

Those were the magic words that pushed me over the top: "good hands." Those were the exact words I had told my father the night before, and now look what had happened to him! My father had had a premonition of this, and by hell or high water, I was going to keep my promise to him that he would wake up from the operation. "Go get me a damn doctor!" I shouted, not caring who heard me. The nurse immediately asked me again to remove myself from the room or she would have me barred. My mother, getting nervous, quietly asked me to wait outside and told me that I was imagining things because I was upset.

I left the room, but before I walked out of the door I said to the nurse, "My father can't breathe! I can hear it. If, God forbid, something happens to him because he can't breathe on his own, you'd better move far, far, away."

By 11 P.M. the doctor stopped by and told us to take my mother home. He said we all should go home and get some rest because we would be no good to my father if we were all exhausted. Hesitantly, we agreed. My mother needed her rest and we didn't want her in a hospital bed next to my father. My sons took Jacqueline home and my brother Michael and I went with my mother. Once at the house, I made her some tea. Just as we were about to sit down at the kitchen table, the phone rang. Michael jumped to answer it. As he listened to the person on the other end the color drained from his face.

"What is it?" I asked frantically, afraid of what his answer was going to be.

"We've got to get back to the hospital. Daddy is having trouble breathing and they had to put him on a respirator," he cried. "He's no longer breathing on his own."

I can't repeat the words that came out of my mouth at that moment, but let's just say they were all expletives. I was so ticked off at that nurse for dismissing me, and if I wasn't so concerned about my father's health, as well as my mother's well-being, I would have gone down to the hospital and wiped the streets with her. I know that violence never gets us anywhere, but this was a life-and-death situation and no one was listening to me.

I kept remembering the promise I had made to my father the night before. "Don't worry, Dad, you'll wake up from the operation." Now it was my job to make sure he woke up. The guilt and fear I felt for my father was beyond words and I didn't know where I would find the answer that would help him, but I knew I had to try to find a way. In contemplation, I looked within. I prayed. I prayed to God and the Universe to please give me a sign that everything was going to be okay . . . any kind of a sign would do. And I got one . . . nothing huge . . . nothing *Aha!* But a sign nevertheless, for at that moment I felt at peace. I no longer felt grief—I felt optimistic! At that moment, I felt sure that he would be okay. Suddenly I just knew that the Universe was going to take care of him. I knew the only thing I could do was surrender and have complete trust in the Universe and my own intuition, that everything was going to be okay. My father would somehow come out of his comatose state, because this wasn't his time—he wasn't ready to pass. I knew that with all my heart and soul. But my father needed help waking from his sleepy haze and I had the chops to do it. After all, I was a fruit peddler's daughter.

When we got back to the hospital they had moved my father into another room that could sustain all the breathing equipment and other monitors they had hooked up to him. The nurse on duty told us he was now in room 217, and my mother, Michael, and I hurried to find him.

As we entered the room, I heard the swishing and pumping of the breathing apparatus as it inhaled and exhaled for my father. I heard the beep, beep, beep, of the blood pressure machine and the clicking of the heart monitor. I couldn't believe this was the same man we had left just over an hour ago. My poor father, he had come to the hospital this morning for a routine procedure and was now lying here on the brink of death. The same nurse who was on call earlier was still there and as she came toward me to speak, I realized I didn't want to waste precious time or energy arguing with her, or anyone else for that matter. What I wanted was answers on my father's condition and what they had planned to get him better. But she dared not ask me to leave the room because that just wasn't going to happen. My family and I promised each other that my father would never be left alone again, not for one minute . . . not until he woke up. One of us, we promised, would always be there for him.

The nurse looked at me apologetically and said in her own defense, "You saw he was breathing on his own."

"Yeah, he was breathing on his own alright, but with difficulty. But what do I know? I'm only his daughter," I said as I turned from her and walked over to my father's bed.

The three of us stayed all night. One of us stayed in his room and the other two slept in the waiting room down the hall. This routine went on for seven days. My father hadn't shown any signs of waking and on the seventh day, the doctor spoke with my mother and me and said we should consider taking him off the ventilator. His chances now of making a complete recovery were extremely slim—only 10 percent. And, he said, if my father did come out of it, he would be a vegetable.

Although I was devastated to hear those words, I didn't believe them. I can only tell you that my instincts weren't telling me to get ready for a funeral. I did sense that my family and I should get ready for a very bumpy emotional and physical journey, but in the end I knew the Universe would take care of my father. This wasn't in the plan for him. No way. And when I spoke with my brothers, they both agreed with me. The doctor didn't know my father. My father was a gambler at heart, and loved a long shot. He was Mikey the Bull. He was tougher than a coma. He would pull through and we would all be there when he woke up. The most important thing that we could do from then on was continue to trust in the Universe and never let go. If we stayed connected to the positive feelings the Universe was sending, he would be okay.

We told the doctor how we felt and he said he understood, but that we should be realistic and look at what my father's medical condition was doing to my mother. My mother was exhausted and hadn't slept in a week. She had been caring for my father since his first stroke some twenty years prior and it was wearing on her nerves. I knew my mother couldn't emotionally or physically deal with this much longer. She spent every moment by my father's side or in the hospital praying for his recovery. My father would have to just wake up and wake up quickly.

Before the doctor left, he said he would be back the following day and we should seriously consider what he had said. He thought it was time to pull the plug, so to speak.

My brothers took my mother out of the room so she could sit and try to take in what the doctor had said, but I stayed behind praying and talking to my father.

"Daddy, please wake up," I said. "Don't you want to go home and have a nice cup of coffee?"

I was at my wits' end. We were running out of time; we were down to *now or never* and the word *never* wasn't in my father's vocabulary, but what more could I do? I kept looking down at my father's face for an answer. It was a rugged face I had looked at all my life, and I realized that although he wasn't breathing on his own and his life was literally being run by machines, I could still feel his massive life force alive and well within the machinery and the wretched bumping sounds of the respirator. Mikey the Bull was living inside and I just knew that the Universe wouldn't let him down, if only we could get him to be one with the Universe again by waking him up.

As I continued to speak to my father, a nun who volunteered at the hospital passed by my father's room, popped her head in, and said, "May I come in and pray with you?"

"Please come on in, Sister," I said. "We could use all the prayers you can muster."

I told the nun what the doctor had said about my father's prognosis. I told her that I wasn't giving up, that I believed God was going to take care of him. I also said that I was sure my father could hear me and I could feel his energy fighting this coma. And I was astounded by her reply.

"I know he can hear you," she said. "In fact, I'm sure of it. What's your father's name?"

I told her my father's name was Mikey and she held my hand and asked me to pray with her. We prayed to St. Jude, the saint of the impossible, to hear our pleas and help my father. Then the nun said to me, "Talk to your father like you would if he were awake. Tell him something that would stimulate his brain to wake up. Come on," she continued. "You can do it!"

"Okay," I said, glad to have found someone who believed in my father's recovery as much as I did.

I quickly scanned my brain as to what to talk about to my father. I figured I'd get tough with him because he was always very strict with us. So I began, "Hey, Pop, I know you can hear me, I can feel you awake inside your sleepy head. But you better get up soon or else the doctor is going to pull the plug. Do you hear me? He's going to pull the plug!"

I waited for a second or two to see if there was any reaction from my father, but there was nothing, no movement whatsoever. I was disappointed and didn't know what else to talk about. Then the sister said, "Talk about things he likes to do."

"Likes to do?" I questioned. "He likes to eat, drink coffee, play cards, and watch television. Oh, and play the horses sometimes at OTB . . . oh, one more thing . . . he loves to play the numbers."

That was it! The numbers! As soon as I said it I felt a tingling sensation go down my neck. And so I began to speak to my father again, this time very quickly and a little louder and with more conviction than before. "Dad," I began, "how about it, do you want us to play a horse for you? If you do, blink your eyes once for yes. Please, Dad, do it now. We'll go play a horse for you, okay?" No response, but I wasn't letting go. I felt a strong energy connection to my father and I could feel his life force, if not his physical body, responding to my voice and my questions.

"Dad," I began again, "your room number is 217. That's a great number, isn't it? Should we go play that number for you, Dad?" I felt myself getting excited. "Michael," I called out into the hallway, "can you come in here for a minute?"

Hearing me yell from my father's room, my mother and brother ran in to see what was the matter. I looked at my brother but continued to talk to my father. "Daddy, Michael is here and he'll go play the number for you. Do you want him to play the number for you? Two seventeen, right? If your answer is yes, blink once now. Please, Daddy, do it for us now. Nobody believes that you can hear us, Daddy. Do it now!"

At that, my father blinked his eyes just once. The screams that came from the hospital room at that moment sent the nurses and doctor running down the hall and into his room. I informed the doctor what had just taken place, but he said not to have our hopes up too high because he believed it was just a natural event, and that my father's blinking had nothing to do with him answering me. I told the doctor not to move, that we were going to try it again, this time with him in the room.

I began again, "Daddy, the doctor is here and he doesn't believe you can hear me. He wants us to pull the plug, Dad. Show him that you can blink your eyes when I ask you to. Daddy, do you want Michael to go play your room number, 217, for you? Blink twice this time if you want him to play it."

Immediately, my father blinked twice and then tried with all his might to open his eyes. The doctor looked at me, my mother, my brother Michael, and the nun and said, "I think he actually heard you."

Feeling relieved and ecstatic, I urged Michael to go downstairs to the gift shop and play the Pick 3 number for our father.

Michael did as my father wanted and put five dollars straight on the number. That night, the number that came out was 217 straight! My father's room number came out and my brother won five thousand dollars, which he needed because he had taken off the whole week without pay.

The next morning when the doctor came in to check on my father, he was amazed to see that not only was my father awake, but he was sitting up and eating Jell-O. Was I surprised? Not for a minute. After all, I knew the Universe would take care of him.

Why? Because I had faith in the signs that the Universe was sending me and I trusted that my feelings were correct, and not just what some naysayers believed—that I was just an overly optimistic daughter who was so fearful of her father's demise that her brain wouldn't allow her to think otherwise. When I recall the days we spent in room 217 with my father, I remember just how hard and scary it felt at times. Yes, sometimes I was scared . . . yet I continued to trust what I was sensing because I had no other choice. I was as sure of what I was feeling as I was sure of my own name, and there was no way I could be dissuaded. Even when I doubted myself for a moment and tried to feel what the doctors were predicting for my father, it just didn't feel right. The sense of it not being his time was too real to be false. It just didn't feel like my father was ready to go, no matter how logically I tried to read the situation. I was in what I like to call a state of total surrender: I first surrendered my feelings and put logic behind me, and then I allowed the Universe to guide us and lend us a helping hand. Remember, surrendering doesn't mean that when you're just too tired of worrying you throw in the towel and say, "I give. I can't take any more." No way. In fact, it is just the opposite. When my father was ill, I was more determined and more zoned into my feelings than ever before. I believed unquestioningly that my father's odds were much better than anyone thought.

When we surrender to the Universe, we only surrender our anxieties, not our wants and needs. Believe me, I'm well aware of just how hard that can be at times. In fact, sometimes surrendering may feel like an everyday battle and a test of your faith, not only in yourself, but also in the higher power. But what I always find is that at the end of the day, no matter if I've strayed in my yielding to the higher power by giving way to my anxieties and becoming fretful, or if I've lost hope or faith in an idea or a pursuit that I believed would work out easily, the answer to my fears is always the same. I go back to the drawing board and make sure I've done all I can do to make the situation work. If I have, I take a deep breath, say a few prayers, and surrender the outcome to God and the Universe. Because if I don't, I won't be able to see the bigger picture when I'm shown it. The outcome—the way it's supposed to be. I must—

we must—surrender in order to achieve our desires, and to literally hear what the Universe is trying to say to us. Which brings me to a lighthearted little lesson I was recently part of at a seminar I was conducting in the quiet little town of Northampton, Massachusetts.

The seminar in Northampton came to me as a fluke. I had no prior plans to conduct a seminar anywhere this summer, especially with the way my schedule looked. I was booked solid for almost the next twelve months. But then one day, my daughter Jackie, who works for me part-time as my assistant, received a phone call from a woman in Massachusetts asking if I could give a seminar there. She knew more than a few people who would love to attend. Although Jackie knew I was booked solid and that I had no time to do it, she still took a shot and asked me if we could give a seminar there.

I looked at my daughter as if she had two heads and replied, "Are you kidding?"

"Come on, Ma, we could consider this a little vacation for the both of us."

"Vacation? Some vacation. I get to book the event, reschedule the clients I already have booked for the weekend, drive five hours—coming and going—and then I get to read . . . gee, let me think . . . probably at least twenty people in one day. Yep, I call that a vacation all right. Are you nuts? You know how booked I am!"

Jackie didn't back down. She said, "I know how booked you are—I'm the one who books you. But there was something in this woman's voice that made me feel we're supposed to do it."

I know some of you are thinking this sounds like pretty good teenage manipulation. But I know my daughter, and this wasn't the case. I knew by the look on her face that she truly believed every word she was saying. So I had no choice but to surrender and say okay and allow the Universe to lead the way, no matter what the outcome or how many people showed up. I wasn't very optimistic about the turnout. After all, I knew no one in Northampton other than the client who called, and I only knew her through my daughter. Of course I had many clients in Massachusetts, but this was the heart of the summer and Massachusetts is a big state. I knew intuitively that it would be a much smaller audience than I was used to, but I surrendered one more time: what I do isn't about quantity, it's about the quality of life and the messages and lessons we receive along the way.

So, two months later, we were off to Northampton. As I had predicted, because of the number of people on vacation and the lack of PR, the ticket sales were less than what I was used to, but we ventured on nevertheless. On August 25, Jackie and I packed my Toyota Avalon and drove from our home on Long Island to Massachusetts, some 210 miles. This would be the first visit to Massachusetts for us both, and we were eagerly awaiting our journey. I was dying to see why the Universe had dropped Northampton into our laps.

This was also our first road trip together. By all means it wasn't our first seminar together, but it was the first time that we had to drive to a seminar ourselves. In the past, one of my sons or someone else had driven me to my seminars. First lesson learned: I was—no, *we* were, Jackie and I—capable of doing it by ourselves.

We left bright and early on Thursday, the afternoon before the seminar. We rested as soon as we checked in to our hotel, which happened to be the same hotel where the event would take place. Heck, we didn't just rest, we conked out for the entire afternoon after we unpacked. In fact, we were so exhausted from our trip that we only got up to eat a little something and went back to sleep. So there went the vacation theory.

The next morning we went out to see the sights of Northampton, but there really wasn't much to see. Northampton is a really lovely little town, with sweet, kind people and an abundance of positive energy, but there really isn't much to do in the way of sightseeing. We had fun, though, shopping in the local grocery store, comparing their prices to the prices at home, then we went to a few other shops and bought some early Christmas presents before going back to the hotel to get ready for the evening event.

Promptly at 6 P.M. the seminar began. As predicted, the audience was small, but they were lovely—in fact, I believe I read almost every person who attended. At the end of the seminar I asked the audience if there was anyone I hadn't read who wished to ask me a question before I had to go. (Jackie and I were driving back home directly after the event that night and although I wasn't by any means rushing the evening, I had to get going while I still had the strength to drive.) A woman sitting on my left raised her hand. I walked over to her and asked her what her question was. She began, "I'm looking to change my career and was wondering if you can see what's the best choice for me."

I immediately saw the word *design* in my head and asked the woman if she'd ever thought about a career in design. She answered that she was a designer by trade and that she wanted to know what path in design she should take.

As I stood there contemplating her answer, and coming up blank, I asked my guides and the Universe to help me give this woman the right direction. Within seconds of my meditation, out of the blue, I as well as everyone else attending the seminar heard a little boy's voice calling from the hallway to his mother. "Mom," he said, "can we go there tomorrow?" Although the event was held at a hotel and it wouldn't have been a shock to hear a child's voice ringing through a hallway, none of us had heard a child's voice until the very moment I stood in contemplation. I knew then that the child was the sign, or the answer to the question I was asking the Universe. I immediately turned back to the woman and said, "Did you ever think of designing things for children?" She paused for a moment, her face flushed, and said, "Why, yes, my dream is to design children's toys!"

"Then that's what your guides want you to know you should pursue," I said. "You're supposed to be doing just that. Don't give up on your dream, because it's about to come true, if you follow through with it and don't lose faith."

What I enjoyed the most about our little seminar was that the people who attended were able to witness how we receive our information from the Universe. When they heard the woman's reply when I asked her if she'd ever thought about designing for children (which I came up with because I heard the little boy's voice in the corridor), the audience was able to put the pieces of the psychic puzzle together along with me and I was able to explain to them where and how I had come to my conclusion.

So remember to have faith in what you believe, and always believe in yourself. Keep in mind that not everyone will always agree with you and your ideas or have the same passions in life that you have, but that's okay . . . you're the only one who has to believe. You and the Universe—and the Universe is always eager, ready, and willing to assist you, just as that little boy's voice assisted me that day with my reading. I asked the Universe and I received an answer in a matter of seconds . . . it was as simple as that. But in order to hear the messages being sent, you have to keep your energy level high as well as your attitude and spirit, even if you break down every now and then. Hey, you're only human. We all break down . . . you should hear me on one of my bad days! But we can't stay down. You must never give up on what your heart and head believe is possible. When you give up on your desires and your wishes, you deplete your energy and the positive vibrations you send out to the Universe. When our energy is depleted it's very hard, if not impossible, for us to hear or see the signs we're being sent.

Remember, success in anything in life isn't easy to attain. If it were, we'd all be Donald Trump, or the American Idol. Everyone has their own stories and journeys they must go through. So while you're writing your own life story, try to maintain a positive attitude as well as positive friends. Don't waste time fighting or complaining about issues or people that really don't matter in your life. Fight for what's worth fighting for: your dreams, your family, your future, and your soul. And when the times come, as they always will, when you feel as though you've forgotten how to surrender, ask the Universe to throw you a life preserver. We all sink now and then in this pond of life, but fortunately we have God, the Universe, the higher power to come to our rescue as our lifeguard, always ready to jump into the rough waters to save us. But first you have to ask for help. So when you feel that you can't beat the tide alone, send out an S.Y.S.—*Surrender Your Spirit*—and allow the Universe to guide you back to shore.

Remember, the Universe is whispering to you, "Have a little faith in me!"

5.

Dear Maury

Always Expect the Best

One of the questions that has perplexed me for most of my professional life as an intuitive is why so many people call and ask me for my advice in helping them redirect their lives, when in actuality they doubt that their lives can be changed or redirected in the first place.

Does it sound absurd that anyone would schedule a reading, wait months for the appointment, pay for their reading, and then ignore or dismiss most of the information they receive? Well, unfortunately it's true. I've taken a mental census and too many of the people who call me don't listen to what they hear or they don't believe that their lives can actually be changed at all.

How can I be so sure they weren't paying attention or taking the direction that they were so desperately seeking? They call me back and usually say something like this: "Hi, Mary, do you remember me? My name is So-and-so, and I had a reading with you last summer. You said that you could see that I was unhappy with my present career and suggested I look for a new one in the medical profession. You recommended anything from a receptionist in a doctor's office to administrative work, maybe as a medical biller. In fact, you even said that you could see me working in a hospital doing just that. You then said that I would meet the love of my life there. Do you remember me now?"

Are you wondering how a client can remember every little detail of what I've told them? Well, it could be because he or she has written everything down or has taped our session, and that's perfectly fine with me. In fact, I recommend it. To be totally honest, most times I don't remember the actual person, but when I get calls like this I ask a few simple questions and their answers usually tell me why they haven't found what they've been looking for.

I begin by asking them something like this: "Sorry, So-and-so, that you haven't changed your career yet and found the love of your life. But may I ask you, did you ever go for an actual interview for a job in the medical profession, or take any courses in medical billing since we last spoke?" Most times the first reply I hear is silence. Then come the excuses, something like this:

"No, Mary, I didn't actually go for any interviews for anything in the medical profession, even though working in a hospital has always been my dream. But I thought if it was meant to be, then it would just come."

That's about the time I literally want to bang my head against my desk. But instead of giving myself a self-inflicted wound, I just say, "Why would you think your life would change just because you want it to? You do know you have to help yourself along the way, don't you?" But I really don't expect an answer to that question. I know intuitively that the real reason why they haven't done anything to help themselves is because some people really don't expect the best things in life to happen to them, no matter what they do, so they don't bother trying.

Another reason for their "why bother" attitude is that they try to look at life logically. Well, logically speaking, I didn't tell this person that she should pursue a career in brain surgery. (But I would have if that was what I had been seeing.) I had told her that I saw that she would be happy with a career in either hospital administration or medical billing.

In all truth, the most common two reasons why people don't pursue the signs they receive are, first, they believe it's just too hard or too much trouble. (We sometimes get into a rut and get used to the limbo state our lives are in, so we don't want to waste time on something we don't think we have the ability to follow through with.) Second, they believe their dreams are just dreams and are more or less just childlike wishes that really can't come true. And even though some feel that way, they still call me because they think it would be fun to see if I can actually read their desires.

I don't mean to sound uncaring, but I wonder why we bother wishing and hoping when most of us assume our wants will go unanswered. I'm sure that before a person calls me, or any other intuitive, they have been praying or wishing for certain things in their life to come true, yet they are doubtful half of them will ever happen. And that really blows my mind. What I'm trying to tell you is not to be surprised or shocked that your prayers and hopes can and actually will come true. So when you make a wish, say a prayer, or talk to your angels or guides, *expect* them to show you a sign to help you find what you're searching for.

Your guides will show you what the outcome will be *if* you take heed and listen to the information you're receiving with an open mind and a positive attitude.

And let's say you've become aware of the signs being sent you and you've jotted them down and still nothing has happened to change your life. Remember that little thing called "free will"? Well, that little thing holds all the power within us. Our free will is the master of the Universe we've created for ourselves. In other words, we hold the keys to the doors of our future. But even though we already have the combination to our own treasure chests, many of us won't allow ourselves to create the new worlds that we say we've been craving.

I believe one of the reasons is because sometimes our thinking becomes blocked. We sometimes feel that all the good things we desire only happen to the other guy. They don't happen to someone like us, the regular stiffs with the nine-to-five job. Well, why the heck not?

Don't be afraid to rock the boat and shake up your logical reality by allowing yourself to dream, and to dream *big*. Don't listen to or become negative with blocked thinking because if you do you'll create and live in a negative universe, and that negative mindset will block all the good things from coming to you.

What do I mean by "blocked thinking?" Blocked thinking is when someone's brain tells them that the information they're hearing doesn't sound logical. Therefore, those people block the idea of something new and different from happening to them because they can't see it for themselves, because the path they're on at the present time is nowhere near the path their guides are directing them to.

The Universe taught my son Carl a lesson about blocked thinking just a few years back.

The year was 1993 and my children and I were living in an apartment in my aunt Margaret and uncle Hugo's three-family home in Ridge, Long Island. My son Carl was a junior in college at Stony Brook University and my daughter Jacqueline was in the third grade at Ridge Elementary School. My oldest son, Christopher, had joined the army a few years earlier and was stationed in Germany. And me, I was diagnosed a few months before with multiple sclerosis. Disabled and homebound, I was usually in so much pain that I spent most of my time flat on my back in bed or on the couch. Because of my physical condition, the job of running the household fell on the shoulders of Carl. It was a difficult thing for any twenty-year-old to handle, but Carl also had to work two part-time jobs while attending college, and on top of that, he worried all the time about me and his little sister. But he was great; he did whatever needed to be done without so much as a whimper. No mother could have asked for a better child.

Carl was so used to caring for everyone else that it was very seldom that anyone, including me, ever heard him complain or saw him frenzied about something he couldn't accomplish on his own. Oh, I'm sure there were times he wanted to pull his hair out of his head with all he had to do, but he usually kept his anxieties to himself because he didn't want to worry me, or for me to feel badly that I couldn't do more for him. But toward the end of the first semester of his junior year back in 1993, I noticed Carl was becoming a bit preoccupied and harried. One night, while he was doing homework at the kitchen table, I heard him sigh deeply.

"Carl, is something the matter?" I asked, concerned.

"Huh? Oh, no, Ma," he answered distractedly.

"You sure?"

"Yeah, yeah . . . I'm fine."

I didn't believe him, but I didn't want to press. If and when he wanted to talk, I'd be there to listen.

Suddenly, Carl looked up and said, "You know, Mom, I wish you still worked for that radio network you used to work for when I was little."

"Why?" I asked. "What made you think of my working at the radio network now?"

I couldn't for the life of me fathom why he would think of a job I had had more than ten years earlier. When I worked for the radio network, Carl was only eight or nine years old, and I had only brought him to work with me a few times so we could spend some extra one-on-one time together. Once when Carl came to work with me, my boss, the vice president and director of radio sales, had his secretary give Carl an envelope with a crisp new five-dollar bill in it for helping me create computer-generated commercial schedules that Carl then distributed to the different departments. But, I wondered, what made Carl think about my old job now, and why did he wish I still worked there? I was sure it wasn't for a crisp new five-dollar bill.

I asked Carl again what made him think of my old job. He said if I worked there, I might be able to help him get an internship. He needed one for his degree and he also knew that an internship would help him get a good job when he graduated. Carl had tried to connect with someone who worked in broadcasting or journalism, but all the doors he knocked on were closed to him. He had called and sent his résumé to local newspapers, magazines, radio stations, and television stations and they had all said that they had hired their quota of interns for the year and there weren't any openings left.

I could hear the defeated resignation in his voice and it broke my heart. If ever I asked my angels for a favor, this was the time. I remember taking a prayer card from my purse that I had been carrying around with me for years. The prayer on the card was by a saint named St. Francis de Sales and it went like this: *Make your-self familiar with the angels, and behold them frequently in spirit; for without being seen, they are present with you.* As I read through the prayer I silently asked my angels and my son's angels to help him with his request.

My son had always been there for me, before and after I had gotten ill, and I was praying and hoping that I'd receive some kind of insightful intuition that could lead him in the right direction to obtain his dearly needed internship. In hindsight I guess I was praying for a sign. I knew that my son had tried all he could do to get the internship the only way he knew how and his energy was completely depleted. And when we become depressed or depleted it's hard for us to see the signs that may be coming our way. So I asked our angels to help me help him. Come to think of it, I think I just wanted to be able to pay him back in some small way, and the only way I could was with my intuition.

Suddenly, an idea popped into my head in the same way I re-ceive information when I'm giving a reading. I received a sudden flash—you could call it an instant replay—of something I had seen just that very morning on *The Maury Povich Show*. While Maury was interviewing someone from his audience he acknowledged one of his college interns sitting next to the guest. Maury made a joke at how many different jobs his college interns did and that working on a television show wasn't as glamorous as it seemed. To-day the intern was a seat filler, sitting in an empty seat in the audience.

"That's it!" I thought. A surge of hope filled my heart. I be-lieved I had an answer to my son's prayers. It was so simple. I was being directed to have Carl write a letter to *The Maury Povich Show*. Seeing that college intern on the show earlier that very day was my sign that Carl should try to get an internship there.

I brought up the idea to my son and his response to me was, "Mom, you can't get an internship on a television show by writing a letter. You have to know someone who works there. But thanks anyway for your input."

Yes, I knew all the reasons why my son would think I had grown another head, but it wasn't that crazy of an idea. I had been giving readings and listening to my guides and sensing the signs I had been receiving for most of my life, and I had learned (the hard way, I might add) that I should never edit what they're showing me. I believe that it was no coincidence that I got the flash of *The Maury Povich Show* I had just seen after I prayed.

But Carl's response wasn't a unique one; most people would have done the same thing. Most of us believe in the logical answer and explanation and ignore the signs we receive. But when we're asking the Universe for help, and receive a sign of what to do, we can't assume it won't work or won't happen just because it's against all odds. Because if we do we'll miss our chance, and if we assume something won't work before we even try . . . well, that's just lazy, pure and simple. In my life, luck, health, and happiness have all been against all odds. Anything I've ever received, I've had the Universe's help in getting it. Geez, "Against All Odds" should be my middle name because that's just what my life has been so far, against all the odds. But it doesn't stop me; in fact, it exhilarates me when the odds are high. I guess that's just the scorpio in me. Scorpios usually want a run for their money, and I've always been a gambler at heart. In fact, if you asked most people who have overcome diversity of any kind, they would tell you it was against all odds that they came through at all.

So I tried explaining to my son that he should at least try out my idea before he threw away what might have been an answer to his prayers. But my words fell upon deaf ears. Carl had made up his mind and he wasn't going to write a letter to a television show, because things just weren't done that way. He was grateful, though, for my concern, but he mentally wrote off my idea as that of a mother grasping at straws trying to help her son with a problem. He had come to the instantaneous decision that things like that never work out, so why even waste time trying and hoping they could be possible?

"Mom, I wish it could be as simple as that, but things like that just don't happen."

"You know why they don't happen, Carl?"

"Why?" he replied.

"Because you don't expect them to."

I felt sad because I knew Carl only had two weeks to get an internship for the upcoming summer and he was turning a blind eye to what I knew was a sign from the Universe. I racked my brain, thinking if I still knew anyone who could be of any help to him in the business, but all my friends had long since left the network. I came to the conclusion that I was losing time trying to figure out things the logical way. I was second-guessing my first sign, and it didn't feel right.

So I went into my son's room and began looking for the tools and the information I would need to try to make the sign I had received a reality. I took Carl's yellow legal pad, which was sitting on his night table, a pen, a recent copy of his scholastic résumé, which was in a file on his bureau, along with some articles he had written for his school paper, in order to create a makeshift press kit for him. I took all the supplies and went into my bedroom and began to write a letter that went something like this:

Dear Maury,

I know you must get tons of letters and requests every day, and I am praying that one of your producers will actually open my letter and read it before it's too late for you or your show to possibly help my son with his dream of becoming a journalist like you . . .

I continued on to say how wonderful and caring Carl was, and that he had a passion for journalism, and how hard he worked maintaining two part-time jobs while still helping me and his little sister. I wrote that he had only two weeks to find an internship before the semester ended, and since it was just days before Christmas, an interview with their show could be the best present I could ever give my son. It would be a boost for his future and proof that all things are possible if we believe. But, I added, I didn't expect him to be hired without an interview. I understood that he would be hired based on his merits as a scholar, and not because of a mother's request. Last, I stated how eternally grateful I was to them for taking the time to read my letter, and I emphasized also how I believed hiring Carl would be beneficial to them because he was such a bright young man and hard worker. Just for good measure, I added that he was really good looking, to boot.

I included a copy of Carl's résumé, his grades, some writing samples, and a copy of his Pride of the Yankees award that he had received in high school for being at the top of his class. Before putting the letter in an envelope I reread it and, satisfied with its contents, I made the sign of the cross, sealed it with a kiss, and asked my guardian angels to carry it to the right hands. I walked to our mailbox and waited for the mailman to arrive and pick it up. I knew his schedule like clockwork; he arrived every day at 1 P.M. As the mailman drove away I said a silent prayer and walked back into the house and waited.

I can honestly say that I was expecting an answer. I always expect an answer because I know that God or the Universe is listening and just waiting for us to ask for help. However, I didn't expect an answer as soon as I received one. Just three days later, the day before Christmas Eve, the call came in.

Carl had gone to Brooklyn to work at his father's restaurant while school was out for the Christmas break. My daughter Jacqueline was still in school, and I was in our apartment alone. When the phone rang, my first thought was that it was someone from *The Maury Povich Show*, but I held my excitement in check. After all, they probably hadn't even received my letter yet. My cousin Roseanne and I had nicknamed our post office "the pony express" because it took so long for mail to go from Long Island to Manhattan and vice versa—sometimes taking up to seven days. We often joked that it would get there faster if we hopped on the Long Island Railroad and delivered it ourselves. So when I picked up the phone, I didn't expect there to be an angel on the other end. A young woman asked if she could speak with Mary Occhino. I said I was Mary. She then said, "Mary, I'm calling on behalf of *The Maury Povich Show* and I'm so sorry it took so long for me to call you, but . . ." Long? I thought. I told her I had just mailed the letter and that she had nothing to apologize for because it was a miracle in itself that she had received it as soon as she had. I also took a moment to tell her how very grateful I was that she took the time to call me at all.

The associate producer—and I wish I could remember her name, but it's a blur—seemed as stunned as I was because she thought she had received it a while ago because it was in an "urgent" pile of letters to be answered on her desk. She went on to say they had just one college internship left and she wanted to know if Carl could get there that day before 5 P.M. for an interview, because the offices and the studio would be closed for the Christmas holiday starting the next day. I think I stopped breathing for a second. It was all so surreal. I quickly told her that my son would be there by hook or by crook, and got the name, address, and phone number of the person Carl was to meet. I thanked the young woman again and as I hung up the phone, I screamed out, "Oh, my God!" at the top of my lungs. I guess I was yelling so loud that my cousin Roseanne, who lived in the apartment above me, ran downstairs to see what was wrong. Poor Ro, I must have scared her half to death with my screaming. When Roseanne finally got to my door she banged and yelled from the other side, "Mary, is everything okay?" Still in my happy delirium I yelled back, "Yeah, Ro, I'm fine, but wait until you hear what happened!"

I opened my apartment door and Roseanne was half laughing and half frightened at my bizarre behavior. Her first words to me were, "Okay, nut, what are you up to now?"

I quickly informed Roseanne about the letter I had written to *The Maury Povich Show* and that someone from his show had just called me saying that they could interview Carl today if he got there before 5 P.M. I looked in my phone book for the phone number of Carl's dad's restaurant. I was happy that Carl was in Brooklyn and not on Long Island when the call came, because the Brooklyn commute to the city was much shorter than the commute from Long Island. Now all I had to do was track Carl down. Finally finding the number, I dialed as my cousin stood back and watched divine intervention at work.

Carl's dad Mario answered the phone and as quickly as I could get the words out, I told him every detail I could remember, from the first time Carl had mentioned needing an internship to someone from Maury's show calling and saying they needed Carl there by 5 P.M. that night. I knew Carl didn't have the right clothes for an interview, so I told Mario we had to do something about it. Mario said he would take care of it; he would bring Carl to the clothing store near his restaurant as soon as he got off the phone with me.

Mario then handed the phone to Carl and I repeated the story all over again, this time to the person who needed to know the most. To say my son was astonished is an understatement. The excited energy that echoed along the telephone wires was priceless. Carl was at a loss for words and in a state of shock. But I told him he had to snap out of it and get moving! The time then was around noon and he still had to go buy the clothes he needed for the interview, take a quick shower, hop onto a train to Manhattan, and get there in time, all the while trying to look as cool as a cucumber. All of which I'm happy to say was accomplished, because at approximately 4 P.M. Carl called me to say he was offered the last internship for the summer season on *The Maury Povich Show*!

I didn't want to say, "I told you so," but I did. I really never had a doubt that it could happen. Not because I'm infallible—because we all know I'm not; no one is. The sign seemed too big to be a coincidence, and we all know what I think about coincidences anyway: I, for one, believe they're tiny miracles in the making.

The irony of this story is that one of the first jobs Carl had to do as an intern was to open the letters from the viewers, which he said came in by the hundreds. And the vast majority were people like me all asking for help. Carl said when he was in the room with the hundreds and hundreds of letters to open, he realized just how miraculous it was for someone to open my letter as soon as they had, just in the nick of time.

Carl's internship taught him many things that summer, one of which was what type of journalist he wanted to be. Carl said he knew then that television journalism wasn't for him, even though he enjoyed working with the staff on the show and he complimented Mr. Povich on being kind to him and everyone else he came in contact with. But he realized newspaper journalism was a better match for him.

More important, Carl learned that when the signs come, no matter how crazy or illogical they may seem, we should follow them. My son also learned that we must expect the unexpected and we must always keep in mind that our intentions, thoughts, hopes, and dreams really do matter. The Universe, God, nature, or whoever or whatever you believe is out there, isn't deaf. Our pleas are heard and the answers often come through signs.

So please don't sabotage your destiny by putting a negative spin to a positive sign or situation. The signs we're receiving aren't just figments of our imagination. Keep your intuition and insight plugged into the Universe and be ready to retrieve the answers that come your way. And don't be shocked when a sudden feeling or thought pops into your head after you've voiced your needs. Be ready to receive the signs being sent, because we are not alone. We are not dancing in the dark; the light of love and hope surrounds us.

6.

Precious Gift

A Promise Made Should Be a Promise Kept

I'm sure you're familiar with the old saying, "Be careful what you wish for because you just might get it." Well, this is especially true if you put your wish out to the Universe. This happened to me a few years ago. I actually made a promise to the Universe, only at the time I wasn't even aware it was a promise. I was simply trying to get my kids to stop bugging me about something they wanted. But the Universe called my bluff and literally made me put my money where my mouth was.

What this experience taught me was that there is always someone out there listening to our pleas, and before we ask God or the Universe for something, we must be ready, willing, and able to accept the responsibility that comes with the gift that we're about to receive. That's the responsibility we have: we have to follow through with the direction given to us with complete blind faith.

Because, as with anything the Universe bestows on us, we choose what we do with our gift. In other words, you can lead a horse to water, but you can't make him drink. Well, that just about sums up my definition of free will. We can ask the Universe for water and the Universe can supply us with it, but it won't shove the water down our throats, even if we're dying of thirst. We decide when and how much we drink.

Often when we make deals with the Universe, we're asking for things we only half expect to receive, and when we get them, we are either too blind to notice, too surprised to act effectively, or too scared to actually move forward. And there are those times when we make promises but we don't expect to have to come through on them. This last scenario reminds me of a funny Burt Reynolds movie entitled *The End*. In one scene, Burt is swimming in the ocean and being pulled down by the undertow; he's exhausted and is convinced he will drown. When Burt finds himself sinking, he starts making promises to God in the form of bribes. At first he promises God that if He helps him swim to shore, he'll donate something like $200,000 to a worthy cause. Then he swims a little further and realizes that he's closer to shore, and that maybe his last offer to God was a little too high. So he lowers the amount of money that he'll donate to $100,000. As he continues to swim (and not drown), Burt keeps lowering the dollar figure until he reaches shore, and he's somehow negotiated the deal down to a couple of hundred bucks.

I remember watching that movie and laughing, not just at how hilarious the scene was, but at how "real" the scene was.

It's so true that art imitates life. I believe that we all, at one time or another, have promised something to God, and when we got what we wanted, we tried to bargain our way out of it. I know I have. I can remember asking God to help me get better. He did, and His help was in the form of intuitive direction. A direction that told me that I needed to watch my diet and stop eating many of the foods I had grown to love throughout my life, like pasta and fried meatballs. He also helped me find the medication that helped me physically go beyond the four walls of my home. But, now that I'm feeling better and I'm able to eat certain things again, I find myself trying to bargain about eating other things. I ask silly things in my prayers like, "Dear God, do you think it's okay for me to have a cookie now?" Can you imagine? A cookie? Realistically, I know that God is busy and that He has better things to do than be in charge of my cookie jar. And yet, every once in a while, I forget how far I've come and how much I've been helped and I try to squeeze in just one more favor. (If you were wondering if He ever answered my cookie question, I would say He has. As soon as I asked, I imagined what His answer would be, and it was, "*Mary, don't push your luck!*")

The truth is, you just can't bargain with God or the Universe. When you make a promise, you have to follow through. And when you wish for something, you have to accept the responsibility that comes when your wish is fulfilled. I'm not saying God is going to strike you down with a bolt of lightning if you try to bargain your way out of a promise. The Universe isn't going to make your world crash and burn because you don't fully embrace the gift it has given you. But an answered prayer is a validation that what you're asking for will be helpful to you, and if you turn your back on it, you lose out and may even harm yourself.

Getting back to the promise I made to the Universe . . . you're probably wondering what it was. I'm going to tell you the story. But first I'm going to give you a little bit of background. As all pet owners know, realizing that your furry loved one may soon cross over is incredibly hard. That unfortunate certainty had been plaguing my family for more than six months. Our much-loved family pet of thirteen years, Sexy, a toy shih tzu, was very ill and was here on borrowed time. She had been blind for two years due to cataracts, and had many other illnesses affecting her health. But this wonderful creature of God never complained once. If there were times when I wasn't feeling well enough to walk her and she needed to go out, she would do so alone by using her sense of hearing as her eyes, very much like a dolphin uses sonar to see. Sexy's sense of hearing was a miracle not only to her, but also for me, because without her acute senses, I wouldn't have been able to keep her as long as I did.

When Sexy needed to go out in the morning, I would just open the side door of my house and tell her that it was okay to walk outside. "Let's go, Sexy, the door's open," I would say. Then I would clap my hands together so she could hear the sound of my hands echoing from the side of the house. I intuitively felt she could judge how far away from the house she walked just by the sound of my clapping. And, as I continued to clap, she would know the distance back to our home. Sexy was our tiny miracle dog, with a heart and soul that were sweet and tender. I still miss her.

Having Sexy in my life taught me that we can learn life lessons from our pets. The life lesson I learned from Sexy was how to have courage. My little toy shih tzu inspired me to face my own sickness. She showed me that where there's a will, there's a way. Even though a person or animal might have a disability, we all can still have a little independence and walk on our own. Remember, animals also have a heart and a soul. And because they love and can be loved, they can also have messages and signs to send to us once they cross over.

When the time came that her body just couldn't go on anymore, my children and I made the decision to bring Sexy to the animal hospital and allow them to help her venture to the spiritual plane. It was a tremendously sad day for my family, but it was especially painful for my son Chris, who was the one who was strong enough to bring her to the hospital. Chris loved Sexy immensely and volunteered to stay with her until she went to sleep.

In the days following Sexy's passing, we still felt her presence around the house. Honestly, it was as if she had never left. Her energy was that strong. The house still had her scent in it. It wasn't the scent of dog fur; Sexy never smelled that way. You see, shih tzus don't have fur, they have hair, and therefore don't give off that doggy kind of odor. I guess if I had to describe the smell that was in the air, I'd say it smelled like Sexy's skin, and the aroma of the lavender-scented dog shampoo I bathed her in.

One morning as I walked through the living room, past the gold recliner that was Sexy's favorite place, I saw her as clearly as I see my own face in a mirror. Sexy was sitting there, in the flesh. She didn't look translucent, like a ghost or a puff of smoke. No, I saw Sexy as she was, cute and rolled into a tiny ball in the corner of her favorite chair, looking straight at me as I entered the room.

I wasn't the only one who saw her in the recliner after her crossing. Chris and Jackie saw her too and freaked out. In fact, after about the third or fourth time she appeared to them, they were so upset that they suggested we get rid of the chair as a way of letting Sexy make her transition to the other side in peace, and I agreed. We didn't think Sexy was an unrested soul, but we did believe she needed help in being released from the physical domain. Sexy needed to be told it was okay for her to go to heaven. (Yes, all dogs do go to heaven.) You see, Sexy's problem was that she didn't understand that she was no longer blind and that she could leave her safe-haven chair. So one last time, I had to direct her the way I had the last two years when she had to go to the backyard to do her business. I clapped. I clapped three times, and then I sprinkled a little holy water mixed with kosher salt around the chair. I told Sexy out loud to go into the light of heaven where she'd be able to see once more. I clapped again, just to help escort her on her new journey, the way I had done so many times before.

After I was done, my children and I waited the rest of the afternoon to see if we could still sense her presence in the chair. When evening came, we realized her presence had crossed. We knew because we could no longer smell her lavender scent around the house. My son Chris picked up the heavy recliner as though it weighed only two pounds, brute that he is, and put it in the garage. We couldn't find it in our hearts to get rid of it that day, but a few months later we donated it to the Salvation Army.

It was approximately six months after Sexy's passing that Chris brought up the idea of us getting another dog. I immediately shot it down. My argument was that I wasn't well enough to walk a dog, and my condition was only getting worse. I said it would be crazy for us to get another dog because I was in no shape to take care of a puppy. Chris found an ally in his sister Jackie, and I had the two of them hounding me (pardon the pun). I stood firm, but they weren't letting up. They even had my little four-year-old grandson Taylor, Chris's son, lobby for them. His response to my veto was, "But, Maremar"—his nickname for me—"we'll take care of the puppy." I didn't have to be psychic to know that there had been some major coaxing going on.

I still wasn't buying it . . . but I must admit I was warming up a bit.

I missed Sexy too, and a new life in the house would be terrific. But there was one additional problem: I didn't have the money to buy a new dog, and I knew I wasn't in any shape to go to the ASPCA to choose one and fill out all the paperwork. I was really that ill. So I compromised and, without knowing it, made a promise not just to my children, but also to the Universe. I said, "If it's meant for us to have a new puppy, then God will just have to send us the money for one."

My children's response was, "Yeah, great, Mom, thanks." I know they believed I answered that way so I didn't have to give them a direct yes or no, and I guess that's exactly what I was doing. But I wasn't thinking that it *couldn't* happen—I just needed a sign that a new dog was meant to be.

Oh, what a sign I would get in about two weeks, when the Universe called my bluff and sent me an announcement.

One of the most miraculous days of my life began on what seemed to be a typical afternoon. At around 1 P.M., I was sitting in my office looking through the mail. As I flipped through the many bills and junk I noticed a letter from the bank I used when we lived in Ronkonkoma years ago. That's odd, I thought. Why would they be sending me a letter now? I thought I closed that account when we moved. Was this some kind of bill?

It seems that my psychic abilities must have gone south for a moment, because my assumption was off by more than a little. In fact, it was off by $8,000! That's right, I said eight grand! It wasn't a bill at all. It was an account statement! Can you believe it? I sure couldn't.

"Eight thousand dollars! Woo-hoo!" I screamed as I limped from my office, trying to find someone in my house to share my amazing news with.

Chris, who had been in the kitchen making lunch for himself and his son, ran from the kitchen toward my screams and asked, "What are you yelling about? Did I hear you scream something about $8,000?"

I showed Chris the bank statement and he said matter-offactly, "So, it's your bank statement. Is there something wrong with it?"

"Yeah, something's wrong; I don't have $8,000."

"Well, call the bank and find out what's going on," answered Chris.

"That's my next step. First I had to let out a scream," I said, laughing.

With that, I went to the kitchen phone and called the bank. I explained, somewhat hysterically, to the person on the other end what I had received, and told her that I had no idea where the $8,000 had come from. I asked if she could help clue me in. The woman started laughing and said, "I'd be kind of hysterical myself if I found out I had $8,000 that I didn't know I had. Give me a minute and I'll check on it."

She put me on hold and I all but held my breath until she came back on.

"Ms. Occhino, it's your money, all right," she said when she got back to the phone.

"Are you sure?" I said with a surprised laugh. "I don't want to start spending money only to find out there was some kind of mistake."

Now, I know what you're thinking . . . if I'm so psychic, how come I didn't know where the money had come from? Why didn't I know if it was a mistake or not? Well, the first feeling I had when I felt the letter was excitement and lightheartedness. What screwed up my intuition was that I used my logical senses to analyze why I was getting a letter, instead of just going with the flow of my first instincts. I've learned when you're dealing with money or legal issues that it's a good idea to make sure of things the old-fashioned way—calling and finding out what's actually going on. But my intuition was telling me it was rightfully mine. I just wanted to back up my assumption with verification from the bank, because if I was wrong, it could be very costly as well as illegal.

"Ms. Occhino," the woman continued, "the money is definitely yours." She then asked me a few personal questions, verifying my Social Security number, my mother's maiden name, and other personal questions. After our Q&A was done, I asked, "Well, do you have any idea where the money came from?"

"It came from Social Security," she answered.

"Social Security? I'm not on Social Security anymore," I replied, confused.

"Well, that's all I know. The $8,000 was direct-deposited into your account the way you used to receive your checks. If I were you, I'd call them and ask them why it's there."

"Absolutely," I said. I hung up the phone, went to my Rolodex, and looked up the phone number for Social Security. I called and asked the caseworker who answered the phone about the money in my account. The caseworker said the $8,000 was definitely mine. It seems they had taken out too much money over the years, and once I dropped Social Security they checked their files and paid me back.

"I was underpaid while I was on Social Security?" I asked, still confused.

"Well, yes, but we knew we were doing it."

Then she went on to explain that it had something to do about me receiving compensation from an accident I had at my job and the payments I got from that. It's complicated, so I won't go into it, but the bottom line was, it was my money and I could do with it whatever I wanted.

I thanked the person from Social Security and told her that I felt like she was my fairy godmother granting me my wishes. As I hung up the phone, Chris, who had been in the kitchen the whole time, asked, "So, is the money yours or what?"

Still somewhat in shock I answered, "Can you believe it? Yes, it's mine!"

"So now we can get the dog!" That was his first reply to my newfound wealth.

"Get a dog?" I hadn't quite digested the fact I actually had an extra $8,000 in the bank. On top of that, getting a dog wasn't the first priority I had for the money.

By now Jackie had come in from outside and Chris informed her about the money. She began jumping up and down and said, "When can we go get the dog?"

"Are you all dog-crazy or what?" I said, somewhat annoyed. "And why are you both busting my chops about a dog?" And then I remembered the promise I had made them a few weeks back. I recalled something else the bank woman had told me, an even stranger coincidence: the money had been in my account for almost a month. So, when I made them the promise that I would buy another dog only when and if God sent the money . . . I already had the money in my account. You see, I might not have been aware of it, but as always, the Universe was. As I said earlier, the Universe called my bluff. It knew something I didn't know, and now it was telling me it was time for me to put my money where my mouth was.

I took a minute to think about if it was wise to spend around $1,000 on a puppy. But then I thought about the synchronicity of events that had taken place in order for me to receive this miraculous money, and I knew that my angels, God, and the Universe would not have made this happen if a new dog wasn't a good idea.

I knew then that the money in my account was a huge sign—heck, it was a billboard—that my words were being heard, and that I was being directed by a higher power. So I told my kids that yes, we could get a new puppy, but with one condition: the dog had to

be female and small like Sexy. I told them that I really wanted a little Yorkie (a Yorkshire terrier), and gave them the go-ahead to find
one they felt was right for us and bring her home.

At the time I was too ill to go to the pet shops with them. Even
if I somehow found the strength one day, I still would not have
been able to go to a pet store because I couldn't take the smells. My
sensitivity to odors was just too extreme. So Chris, Jackie, and my
grandson Taylor got into my son's truck and drove around to different pet shops all over Suffolk County, looking for puppies. I
didn't know who was more excited—Chris, Jackie, or my four-
year-old grandson. When I watched them pull out of the driveway
with huge smiles on their faces, it felt like Christmas in June. To a
mother and a grandmother, looks like that are priceless.

As they entered each and every pet store, they'd call me to let
me know what kind of puppies were in stock. They hadn't found
any Yorkie pups yet, but they were having a great time playing
with and enjoying all the new puppies they were meeting.

Their last stop of the day was at a pet shop in Port Jefferson, a
town on Long Island known mainly for its ferry and many hospitals. In fact, Jackie and Taylor were both born in a hospital in Port
Jefferson. Chris called me one last time and said somewhat excitedly, "Mom, this store has Yorkie puppies and Jackie and I have
narrowed it down to two of them. But we'll leave it to you to make
the decision on which one comes home."

"Thanks," I said. "Not too much pressure."

I asked Chris to hold the puppies up to the phone so I could try
to zero in on their energy. He did as I asked. Then I asked him,
"One is a boy and one is a girl, right?"

"Yes," he admitted. He hadn't told me beforehand that he had
one of each sex because he wanted me to choose without knowing
prior.

"Put the first puppy by the phone."

Chris put the first puppy near the phone and then the second. I made him do it one more time without saying a word, and then I asked, "Does one have curly hair?"

"Yes," he said.

"That's the one I want."

"Yeah!" I could hear my daughter Jackie chanting in the background.

"Is the curly-haired one Jackie's favorite?" I asked, smiling.

"Yes," said Chris a little solemnly.

"And is the curly-haired one the girl?"

"Yes," he answered.

"Great, wrap her up and take her home."

A short time later, my three pet shoppers found their way home with the newest four-legged member of our family. We all tried to come up with a name for her. We first thought about naming her Rosie, after Grandma Rosie. Then Jackie put her down on the floor to let her walk. She was only six weeks old and weighed just a pound and a half. To see her hop around like a little bunny was absolutely precious, and that's exactly how my daughter described her.

"Mommy, isn't she precious!"

"That's it, Jackie, you've got it. That's our dog's new name, Precious!"

Precious had found her new home. I mentally asked Sexy if she would help Precious get acquainted with us and her new home. I have no doubt that Sexy did just that, because after we got Precious there were more Sexy sightings.

But that's not the end of my promise story . . . no, I still had more lessons to learn from the Universe. Precious was doing fine, and we were all getting used to having a new baby in the house.

But after the first few days of trying to keep up with her and becoming exhausted, I realized I had to fence her in. I decided to limit her walking space to the hallway between my and Jackie's bedrooms and the bathroom, which was about a fifteen-foot walkway.

I bought a baby gate online from Babies R Us and hooked it up to where my bathroom ended and the living room began. The only problem was, every time I had to pass I had to open the gate, and Precious would make a mad dash between my legs. She'd run out, and I'd have to capture her all over again. This little precious pound-and-a-half puppy was ruling the roost. I must say, if I wasn't so tired running after her (or I should say, tired of attempting to run after her), I would have found the whole situation very funny.

My daughter Jackie suggested that I lift up my leg and climb over the gate the way she did when she wanted to pass. I remember looking at her like she had two heads when she made that suggestion.

"Lift my leg over the two-and-a-half-foot gate? Do you live here?"

"What do you mean, do I live here?" Jackie asked.

"I mean just what I said. Do you live here?"

"Yeah, I live here. What are you trying to say?"

"What I mean is that you know I can't even lift my left leg six inches, so how am I supposed to lift it two and a half feet over the gate?" As if anticipating her next suggestion I said, "And if I lift my right leg, my left leg won't support my weight."

I know I sounded nasty answering my daughter the way I did, but I was trying to be as truthful as possible and not sugarcoat the way I was or how I felt. I felt trapped in a body that no longer worked the way it used to. I was frustrated that everyone didn't realize just how much I couldn't do anymore, and I must admit, sometimes I took it out on the people I loved the most and who did the most for me. I want to take this opportunity to thank my children for always being there for me when I needed them, and allowing me to sound off on them at times when they didn't deserve it. I'm so very sorry and I thank God for you every day.

What got me so infuriated wasn't my daughter's suggestion, but my own limitations. My last MS attack, on New Year's Eve 2000, had been the most devastating episode to date. That attack left me in bed and immobile for over three months and took at least 40 percent of the strength from my left side. This was June of the same year. I was still getting used to my new physical restrictions and it ticked me off.

Jackie understood what I meant, but continued, "Okay, you can't lift your leg that high. But have you tried lately?"

"No," I answered honestly. But I knew how tired and weak my leg would get just walking from my bedroom to the kitchen; I also knew how sometimes my leg would drag because it was so numb. The thought of lifting my leg sounded totally absurd. But I knew it was important to my daughter, so I tried.

My first attempt was hard. In fact, the only way I could get my leg over the gate was if I grabbed hold of the bottom of my slacks and used the pant leg like a pulley for my leg. It was a lot of work and sometimes painful, but . . . it was working. After a while, I no longer needed to grasp my slacks to help pull my leg—I was lifting my leg by myself with the use of my muscles. It was a struggle, but I was doing it. By the third and fourth week of lifting my leg over the gate, I could do it as well as anyone else in the family.

The miracle of it was that the dog's gate became my physical therapy. I was getting better, or at least the strength in my leg was. I was walking better, with more stamina, and I had more energy than ever before. All because I had to care for our new puppy Precious.

I know our new puppy was a sign that Sexy was not only trying to help me heal from my grief of losing her, but also helping to heal me of my mental and physical limitations.

So if you ever make a promise, be ready to make good on it, because once you do, the possibilities of enhancing your life are endless. Know that sometimes our prayers are being answered before we've even mouthed a word. Most important, remember that a promise made should always be a promise kept, because our prayers and wishes are promises we are wishing for ourselves.

7.

Six Degrees to John Edward

Your Possibilities Are Endless

The year 2000 was both the best of times and the worst of times for me. The bad stuff started right at the beginning, on New Year's Eve. While most of the world was celebrating the beginning of a new century, I had the most severe MS attack of my life, which temporarily left me partially parlalyzed as well as bedridden for a few months. One of the best times was when the television show *Crossing Over* aired that same year. I loved that show. The first time I watched it, I was so happy I felt as if I had died and gone to heaven. Finally, I thought, there was a psychic medium on television who didn't sound like a cheerleader calling out letters when he gave a reading. (In the past, most of the psychics I had seen, especially ones known to be "psychics to the stars," always seemed to come up with just initials and very few names when they gave readings. Hence the nickname "psychic cheerleaders.") Now, I'm not saying that I've never seen John Edward give initials on TV, or that I've never given initials myself in a reading. But when I saw John give first and last names the way I did, I knew I had found someone very like myself. I couldn't wait for his show to air every day. Lying in bed, unable to do much of anything, I had very little to look forward to, until *Crossing Over* came on the tube.

I didn't miss an episode, and I began studying John and how he controlled his intuition. In fact, I was reading him as he zeroed in on certain people and I was thoroughly impressed by how he controlled his focus, even though there was an audience full of people surrounding him, all praying to be read. John made it look easy, but as a psychic medium I'm telling you it's not.

I wasn't watching John because I was trying to copy his style; I was focusing on his sense of concentration and the audience's responses. I was taking mental notes on how I would someday read my audiences, if God gave me the strength, and how I would conduct my seminars across the country. I didn't want to do it for the accolades, mind you—all I wanted was to be able to offer comfort to many clients at once instead of just one at a time, the way I had been doing over the phone. I was amazed at how accurate and at ease John seemed to be with so many people at one time, and I couldn't wait to do it too.

As I said before, during the time I was observing John, I was totally disabled with multiple sclerosis; and I hadn't seen a client face-to-face in nearly three years. But, for some reason, when I watched his show I felt the show itself was a sign of things to come for me. When I saw how much it did for the people who came and were lucky enough to be read, I knew I had to try to help, the same way John and other psychics like George Anderson were doing. I wanted to be part of an army of psychics who helped people all over the country, not only by giving readings and connecting them with their loved ones, but also by teaching them how to connect with the Other Side themselves. I knew I was helping people through my phone readings, but somehow, it just didn't seem like enough anymore—I felt I was supposed to try to reach many more.

In case you're thinking I was suffering from delusions of grandeur, hoping I would be the next "psychic star," I guarantee you I wasn't. I wasn't thinking that I had to have my own TV show. I didn't want to be a celebrity psychic. I just wanted to have the strength to do my work . . . period.

John's show was a sign of hope to me at a very bleak time of my life. It was a sign that I wouldn't be a captive in my home for the rest of my life—his show made me believe that I would regain my strength and become mobile once more. You could say his show allowed me to do a reading on myself, without even trying. All I can say is that I felt a certainty about my future after I began to watch John Edward, and mentally began making plans and setting goals for my future. For that, I am eternally grateful.

I never mentioned my intentions or my wishes to anyone. But one day, as Jackie and I were watching his show together as we usually did, she said, "Mom, too bad you can't get out of the house the way you used to, because you could be reading all those people like he does."

I said nothing but thought, "Out of the mouths of babes." My daughter had read my intentions before I had uttered a single word. Jackie had the same feelings as I had, but she just was too young to understand them thoroughly. I knew she would in time. After her comment, I told her how on target she was. I told her that I could "see" myself giving seminars. I also divulged to her that I had whispered my intentions to the Universe for safekeeping, and that all that was left for us to do was go about our lives and be ready for a sign from above. Jackie just smiled. I know she believed I could get better—she never really accepted my being ill anyway. She always made me push myself when I thought I couldn't push any further. So when I acknowledged my dreams, they didn't seem so far-fetched to her either.

A few days later, as I was watching *Crossing Over*, a few more people became privy to my intentions. Jackie came home from school with some giggling girlfriends prancing behind her, making lots of noise. I told the girls to try to lower their voices because I was doing my homework. One of Jackie's friends, whom I had never met before, giggled, tapped my daughter on her shoulder, and asked, "What kind of homework is your mother doing? She's watching TV."

Jackie told her friend that I was a psychic like John Edward, and that I was studying the way he read his audience.

"My mother tries to read certain people in his audience before he gets to them. She writes down what she feels and then she sees how well she's done when he gets to read them."

"Why?" asked her young friend.

"Because my mom says she's getting ready for when she goes on tour around the country giving seminars."

"On tour?" the girl exclaimed. "I thought you said your mother was sick and hardly ever left the house!"

"She is sick," answered Jackie. "And she doesn't go out much, but she says she'll be able to do a lot of things someday."

I knew the girls didn't want to laugh out loud at my fantasy of going across the country reading people. They were trying to be kind, but I knew inside they thought I was merely dreaming. And in all honesty, I understood how the girls felt. But I wasn't laughing, because I knew, and my daughter knew, that I was serious . . .

as serious as a toothache. We both just let it go and didn't discuss it further in front of other people. But Jackie knew that I was watching *Crossing Over* as research for my future.

I want everyone to know: I was realistically aware of how high the odds were stacked against my ever pursuing a career as a psychic medium outside my home because of my illness. I had multiple sclerosis, and I was getting worse with each attack. That much was a fact. Nevertheless, as I've said before, my entire life has been against all odds. And now, having this new focus and these new intentions . . . it felt so right. It wasn't hard for me to surrender to my expectations, because I've always believed in the impossible and in miracles. Hey, I had seen them happen before in my life! I knew this wasn't too huge for the Universe to handle. And you know what? When you expect a miracle, you receive a miracle; it's as simple as that.

I guess surrendering to my expectations came easier to me than to others, because I had taught myself throughout my life not to edit my thoughts or feelings, no matter how improbable they seemed. The Universe didn't give me a time frame for my physical breakout. But in all honesty, I wasn't anxious about when or where my miracle would take place. I surrendered to my wish, and to the idea that when it was meant to be, it would be. In the meantime, I continued to watch John's show. I did my homework and got ready for "someday."

And someday came sooner than even I ever expected.

My "someday" started with a domino effect of coincidental events—a set of synchronistic occurrences sent by the Universe to show me the way to my future. It began the day I received a call from Gary Schwartz, Ph.D., author of *The Afterlife Experiments* (which, by the way, wasn't published at the time, so I had no idea who Gary Schwartz was). I would later realize that Dr. Schwartz was the first degree in my six degrees to John Edward, and part of the Universe's plan for getting me out of my house and into the public arena.

It was February 2001 when Gary Schwartz first called me for a reading. As I said, I had no idea who the man was. To me he was just another person who found me through word of mouth. But, to make a long story short, I read Gary and he said he was impressed with the reading, and asked if I'd like to be tested by his associates in the same way they'd tested John Edward, among others. Was I stunned that this man had tested John Edward and George Anderson? Yes, for about a minute . . . then I got over it. Don't get me wrong, I was plenty amazed that Gary Schwartz somehow found me—a woman who almost never left her home. But I also believe in miracles with all my heart. So I happily and gratefully agreed to be tested by Dr. Schwartz.

A few months after Gary and I had met and I had gone through some extensive psychic testing, which consisted of double-blind studies with many other therapists, psychologists, and doctors, I received a call from a woman in California who said that Dr. Schwartz had recommended she call me for a reading. After our session was through, she said that she was one of the first people who had been involved in helping John Edward get started giving seminars, and she wanted to know if I was open to the idea of holding seminars too.

"Of course," I said not thinking for one moment about my physical condition. At the time of her call, I was still so fatigued that I really didn't know how or where I would find the strength to get out of my house, never mind conduct a seminar. But I wouldn't allow my illness to block what the Universe might be sending, so I went right ahead and asked her just where she wanted me to give this seminar.

"California," she said nonchalantly. "Is that a problem?"

"Well, you mentioned you were recommended to call me by Gary Schwartz, right?" I asked.

"Yes," she answered.

"Did he happen to mention to you that I have multiple sclerosis?"

"Yes, he did," she answered. "But you sound okay to me . . . do you think you'll be able to do it?" she continued.

"Oh yeah, I'm sure," I said as I swallowed hard. Talk about your surrendering. At that moment, I had no idea just how or where I would find the strength or stamina to carry out the task that the Universe had laid at my door. But I knew I wasn't supposed to question it. I instinctively knew help was on its way—it just had to be. I couldn't believe that God or the Universe would bring all these little miracles to me and then allow me to be disillusioned. No—I had faith that I read the signs correctly, and just concentrated on keeping my eyes open to see what was lying ahead for me.

Remember the old saying I mentioned in the last chapter: "Be careful what you wish for because you just might get it!" Well, I sent my intention of being able to give seminars out to the Universe months earlier, and now like a boomerang it was coming back to me. I asked for it and I got it. I wasn't supposed to be afraid, and I wasn't (though I was a little bit nervous about flying, after not being on a plane for nineteen years). I was just going to trust the journey the Universe was arranging.

So, a few weeks later, I was off to California to conduct my first seminar—which coincidentally was in the same exact place where John Edward conducted his first seminar.

But my miracles didn't end with that woman's call. In fact, soon after I received another miracle that really made me able to go to San Diego to give that seminar. Not long after we spoke, I heard about a medication that I believed would help me get better. It was called Prokarin, a topical cream created by Elaine DeLack.

God was really being good to me, I thought. But I was having a hard time getting a prescription: my regular doctors wouldn't write the prescription for me because the medication still wasn't approved by the FDA to be used for patients with MS. (The ingredients were approved separately, but not together for the purpose of helping a person with MS.)

So, what did I do? I did what anyone who wants to try a new medication does when they're having trouble getting a prescription . . . I called the inventor. Elaine DeLack is a kind and compassionate woman who wasn't bothered by my call. In fact, she speaks every day to MS patients who are searching for help. Elaine gave me the phone number of a compounding pharmacist named Howie on Long Island who was trained to produce Prokarin. Howie in turn introduced me to Dr. Julius Bazan.

At this point, I thought the Universe was really testing my surrendering skills and seeing just how much I actually wanted a new life. I won't lie and say that there weren't moments when I felt like I was driving down a dead-end street, chasing after doctors everywhere. But fortunately, those sullen moments didn't last too long. I still knew how I felt inside, so I continued my quest.

The next day I made an appointment with Dr. Bazan; the day after that I was sitting in his waiting room with my son Chris, filling out new patient medical forms. I eventually got down to the question I was a little leery about filling in: occupation. "Oh boy," I thought to myself. "Here we go again. Here come the snickers." Snickers, mumblings, laughter, and jokes had followed after I returned my forms to the medical receptionists at other doctors' offices. And I was really getting tired of defending what I did for a living to skeptics. So, before I filled in the occupation blank, I told Chris what I was contemplating filling in: "None of your business."

Chris shook his head and said, "Mom, don't deny what you do; you have nothing to be ashamed of."

"You know, Chris, you're right," I said with newfound confidence. So I filled in the occupation question with *psychic medium* and waited for the chuckles to begin after I handed the form to the doctor's secretary. But to my pleasant surprise, the chuckles never came. What did come was a statement I never thought I'd hear in a zillion years.

"Psychic medium?" said the secretary behind the desk. "Isn't that a coincidence? My husband works for a psychic medium."

"He does?" I asked, a little stunned. "Who?"

Now you might be thinking, "Hey, she's a psychic, she's supposed to know if someone's pulling her leg." Well, that's not true. Oh, it's true that I'm a psychic, but it's not true that I read everything and everyone every minute of the day. I'm not God; I'm just a person with a good intuitive antenna. In my own defense, I find it very hard to read people if I'm nervous or anxious about things affecting my life. Trying to get a prescription for a medicine that was still more or less experimental was major and possibly life-changing. And after having gone to four other doctors who all told me no, the last thing I was focusing on was reading this doctor's secretary.

"I'm sure you've heard of him," she continued. "He's got that new show on TV called *Crossing Over*."

"John Edward?" I asked, as I felt my blood pressure rise with excitement.

"Yes," she replied. "That's him."

"What does your husband do for John Edward?" I asked.

"He's the technical director of the show," she answered proudly.

At that very moment, I knew I was in the right place at the right time. I also knew this woman's lack of cynicism was a sign that Dr. Bazan would be willing to write the prescription for me. Most important, I believed the fact that everything was working out so seamlessly was a sign that the Prokarin would work for me. After she told me her husband worked on John Edward's show, I just knew it was meant to be.

John Edward was one of my earth angels and he didn't even know it. But I knew—I knew from the first time I watched his show. I could sense John was going to affect my life in a big way, and by God he did.

But the synchronicities connecting me with John Edward didn't end there. There's more—much, much more. Even now, I can't even begin to explain to you just how in awe I was of the Universe and of all my angels. As I recall these events today, I'm still blown away.

A few months down the line, after I had given my first seminar in California, I was introduced to an editor at Penguin named Denise Silvestro. Believe it or not, Denise just happened to be the editor of John Edward's first book, *One Last Time*. And Denise wound up being the editor of my first book, *Beyond These Four Walls: Diary of a Psychic Medium*. Finding Denise was another miracle, one that I thank God for every day. It all came about through a woman named Christine Dumas who is now one of my closest friends in the world.

But back to the story. Can you believe it? I went from being a woman who was totally disabled with MS—a woman who wasn't able to leave her home for months at a time—to a touring psychic medium conducting seminars across the country, to an author traveling on book tours across the United States.

Have you had enough miracles for one chapter? Wait, there's one more. . . .

In August 2002, I was scheduled to do another seminar in San Diego, California. This time, my son Carl escorted me. Although I was already on Prokarin and more or less back on my feet, I was still kind of weak and really couldn't travel alone.

So, on August 24, 2002, Carl and I flew to San Diego. After we landed and settled into our hotel rooms, we ate dinner. Afterward, Carl and I stood outside my room on the balcony and looked at the beautiful San Diego sky. Suddenly and very nonchalantly I turned to my son and said, "San Diego is really beautiful. No wonder Joanne moved here."

"Joanne? Joanne who?" Carl asked.

"You know what Joanne I'm talking about," I said, making him think a little harder.

"Yes, I think so," he said after a second or two. "Charlie and Renee's mother, right?"

"That's her," I acknowledged.

Charlie and Renee are my niece and nephew; Joanne, their mother, was my brother Charles's first wife. I hadn't seen any of them in twenty-six years. I had a chance to speak with my niece sixteen years prior, but I had completely lost touch with her since then. My brother Charles hadn't had any contact with either one of them in just about the same amount of time. But they were never out of our minds. Not one holiday, not one birthday, not ever . . . and we missed them so much it hurt just thinking about it.

Suddenly, after thinking about Joanne, I got a gut feeling that I should just pick up the phone and dial information and see if we could track her down while we were there. In hindsight, I realized that I didn't have to wait to dial 411 in San Diego—I could have done it back in New York. But for some reason, it felt right doing it there. It was just meant to be. I dialed information and asked for Joanne (and I intuitively gave the operator her maiden name). I took a shot after not hearing or seeing her in all those years that somehow she would be listed under her maiden name, and you know what? She was!

The operator found her number immediately and gave me her *listed* phone number . . . another miracle! I immediately dialed the number. To my disappointment she wasn't home, but I was happy to know that I had the right Joanne because I heard her familiar voice on her answering machine. It hadn't changed a bit in all those years. I left a message on her machine saying it was me, Mary Saliba (my maiden name). I told her that I was in San Diego on business, and gave her the name of the hotel where I was staying. I took a shot that she didn't hate me and that maybe she would call me back. And I'm happy to say she did just that. About a half hour after I called her, she returned my call. Our conversation went something like this:

"Hello, Mary?"

"Yes . . . Joanne?"

"Yes!" she exclaimed.

"*Oh, my God!*" we both screamed.

Our conversation went on and on as we tried to catch up on a quarter of a century in a ten-minute phone conversation. Finally, I asked Joanne if she'd like to come to our hotel so we could sit and talk in person. Joanne agreed, and within an hour Carl and I were hugging her. My angels are fierce and so on target. As it turned out, Joanne only lived a short distance from our hotel and was just as excited about seeing us as we were about seeing her.

Joanne brought us up to date on her children and told me that I was now a great-aunt. Renee was married and had a beautiful little girl named Madeline. And my brother Charles, Renee's dad, was a grandfather for the first time. I could hardly catch my breath. I was in awe of how lucky I had been, how miraculous the Universe was, and how wonderfully life was treating me.

We made arrangements to meet with Renee the following day, but my nephew Charlie, I'm sorry to say, wasn't available.

The following day my niece came by our hotel. I can't put into words the overwhelming sense of astonishment I felt when I saw her. But the best was yet to come, because after we spoke and hugged and kissed a million times, Renee did yet another miraculous thing . . . she called her father from my hotel room and said the words my brother had been waiting to hear for almost sixteen years.

"Hello, Daddy, it's me, Renee!"

John Edward, wherever you are, God bless you. It all began with you and the feeling I received when I watched your show and studied your audience.

If anyone who reads this chapter still doesn't believe that synchronous coincidences are miracles in the making and that the possibilities in your life are endless, I don't know what else I can say to convince you otherwise. I'll only leave you with this . . . start to pay attention to your life, and study its rhythms. Make sure you take note of the signs you receive while on your journey. You'll be amazed at the infinite amount of miracles you'll receive, and the never-ending possibilities that life will offer you!

8.

Grandma, Can You Hear Me?

Sometimes Even Psychics Need a Psychic

There are some people in the world who think psychics are magicians—that we can change people or situations with the snap of a finger or the twinkle of a nose. Well, we're not. It's true that psychic mediums can communicate with the dead and connect with what some call the Other Side. But really, we are just regular people who have an extra sense of intuition, commonly known as a sixth sense or ESP (extrasensory perception). Most of us are born with five senses: sight, sound, smell, taste, and touch. The sixth sense is what I describe as a mental antenna raised a little bit higher than normal, making it easier for those who have it to connect with the energy surrounding them. Sometimes this sixth sense is insight into the future or into the spirit world; sometimes it's just a better grasp of everyday feelings and emotions. My sixth sense has allowed me to be a spiritual broadcaster—an announcer, if you will—for those in the spirit domain. One who can interpret messages, signs, and information.

But psychic mediums are human beings, just like you. We have the same human responsibilities, frailties, and fears. And just like you, we have our breaking points—the moments when grief and despair fill our every waking hour, when we begin to doubt everything we have ever known to be true, and even ourselves. Such a time came for me about eleven years ago, in 1994, after my grandma Rosie passed on.

Grandma Rosie had been dead for a little over three months, and I missed her terribly. I hadn't seen much of her the last year of her life, and I was grief-stricken that I would never have the chance again. You see, the last year of Grandma's physical life was the first year I started dealing with my own illness, which meant that I hadn't been able to drive into Brooklyn the way I used to. The cruel fact was, my illness had kept me away from my grandmother for seven months—longer than I had ever gone without seeing her before in my life. And now that she was gone, I felt my life would never be the same.

One particularly bad day, as I was lying in bed, I started thinking about everything Rosie had meant to me and my family. Grandma had been the glue that held us together. As little as she was, she always seemed to be able to rein us in with her no-nonsense tact. I recalled all the wonderful holidays I had shared with my aunts, uncles, and cousins, with little Rosie at the helm, and I began to fear that the days of our family get-togethers had passed the same day Grandma did. On a personal level, I felt like I had lost one of my best friends in the world. You see, Rosie really got me. I was never odd or different to her. She encouraged me to follow my intuition, accepted my flaws, and wasn't afraid or too shy to tell me when I was acting like an idiot.

One of the things Rosie always told me was, "Keep your eyes and ears open." But she didn't mean my physical eyes and ears; she meant my intuitive eyes and ears. Because she supported my gift, I always felt comfortable talking to her about what I should do with my life and my intuitive skills. Grandma really understood me and, in fact, we were a lot alike. For one, we both married very young and had children at an early age. Grandma was only sixteen when she gave birth to my mother, and I was eighteen when I gave birth to my first son, Christopher. Grandma was also very independent and worked most of her life, marching to the beat of her own drum. She was for women's lib long before that term came along. I saw how she took the bull by the horns, as she would say. She never waited for life to come and find her—she was a leader, not a follower. And she couldn't care less whether or not you liked it. I know it was Rosie who made me the way I am . . . independent.

My mind drifted to the sound of Grandma Rosie's voice answering the telephone. "Hell-lo," she would say, sounding more like she was singing a song than just answering a ringing telephone. That is, if she was in a good mood. If you caught her on a bad day, you'd know it immediately: she'd answer with a curt "Hello!" (You didn't need to be psychic to read Grandma!) At times like that, I knew I had two choices: I could tell her I'd call back later when she didn't sound so busy (sometimes the wisest thing to do) or I could stay on the line and ask her what was wrong. If Grandma didn't want to discuss something, she would tell you straight out. And if she did decide to talk, you'd better be ready to hear what she had to say, good or bad, because she'd tell you just what was on her mind.

Come to think of it . . . Grandma was an awful lot like me, or vice versa.

But getting back to the story . . . That morning, I was feeling lower than I ever had before. I was grieving not only for my grandmother, but also for the changes that had occurred in my life. So many things had happened to me in the last year. I was grieving for the Mary I once knew, who had now been replaced by a weakened stranger.

I felt very unsure of my destiny, like a stranger in my own body. My illness was leaving me weaker and weaker, and my attacks were lasting anywhere from six weeks to three months. True to my diagnosis, the attacks would come and go. But although I'd get better after each episode, it could take months for me to get back to where I was *prior* to the attack.

Each episode was taking away a little part of me. Each time I ended up less capable and strong than I was before.

Tossing and turning, I forced myself to close my eyes, and began reciting my rosary the way I do when I can't sleep. Eventually I dropped off. And right away, I started dreaming about my grandmother. I could see her in her living room on East Eighth Street in Brooklyn, sitting in her little wooden rocking chair with yarn in a basket on the floor beside her, crocheting a baby blanket while watching television. And I saw myself sitting on her couch and she looked right at me and said in her no-nonsense tone I knew so well, "Knock it off!" Grandma could never stand for any self-pity b.s. She also knew that I rarely indulged in feeling sorry for myself—I was too much like her, and she never gave up. Then, in my dream, I started talking to her the way I'd done hundreds of times before. I was telling her that I missed her. I was finally acknowledging to her and to myself how sad I felt about being diagnosed with multiple sclerosis—something I had never said before, even in my sleep. In our waking hours, it is much easier to put on a brave face and fake a positive attitude, but when we're alone with our fears, it's much more difficult. I've learned that there's no better place for us to face our fears, demons, or uncertainties than in our dreams, and that was exactly what I was doing.

I also asked my grandmother for a sign that she had made her transition to the next phase of life okay. I wanted validation that I'd still be able to communicate with her as I had done with so many strangers through my readings.

As a psychic, I should have known that this was no ordinary dream. Everything was clear and seemed so real; and when you have a dream like that, and remember it all when you wake up, chances are it was actually a visitation from your loved one. And this "dream" about Grandma Rosie couldn't have been more real. Here I was, receiving the biggest sign I could ever get, and I didn't even realize it. I was actually connecting and communicating with my grandmother.

You would also think that as a psychic I should have known that people who pass remain connected to their loved ones in the physical world. And I *did* know Rosie was still connected to her family. But the fact remained, I hadn't "heard" from her, so to speak, since her passing and I found it very upsetting. I guess what I was requesting was a little extra attention from her—a personal express telepathy that I knew she was capable of sending. And I asked her to help me find the strength I had inside to help me get better. I knew eventually my anxious state would pass. But in the meantime, I asked her if she could send me some kind of a physical sign to let me know she was still connected.

It's times like these when a psychic needs another psychic.

After a few minutes, I awoke from my visit with Grandma. I must admit, I was feeling a lot more optimistic. I said another Hail Mary just for good measure, and sat up in bed, refreshed and enthusiastic. Then, as I bent over to look for my slippers, I began hearing music. I wasn't sure where it was coming from: I hadn't set the radio alarm clock, so the music couldn't have been coming from there. No, this sounded more like a melody from a music box. As I listened more closely, I began to make out the tune . . . "Raindrops Keep Falling on My Head."

How appropriate, I thought. After all, I had just been feeling sorry for myself.

I looked around my room to see where the music was coming from. My dresser . . . there the little stinker was! A little brass musical sculpture of a deer. It had been a birthday present from my aunt Suzanna. She had known that I collected music boxes, and she said when she saw it and heard what song it played, she decided it would make a nice gift for me. But why would it be playing right now? Curious, I got up and walked over to the dresser to check it out. I turned the little brass deer upside down, looking for any malfunctions that would make him go on his own. I couldn't remember the last time I had actually played it, and I had to remind myself how to turn him on: a lever on the base of the statuette about an inch long. Moving the switch from right to left turned the deer on, and sure enough, it was all the way to the left.

I switched the lever to the off position, thinking to myself how sticky it was, and went back to look for my other slipper under my bed. And as I was on both knees, I tried to figure out how the figurine could have possibly turned on by itself. I may be psychic, but I don't believe that *everything* has a paranormal explanation. Perhaps the lever hadn't been completely turned off—a passing car or truck, or even someone jumping upstairs, could have caused just enough vibration to slide it into the on position.

Nope. I quickly realized both possibilities were logically wrong. First of all, I was the only living soul in a twenty-one-room house. Nobody was doing any jumping.

Second, the house I was in was on a cul-de-sac—a dead-end street far from a main intersection or heavy traffic. Heck, the house was on two acres of land, and there were only four houses on the block. And, I might add, it was not even 7 A.M. on a Saturday morning in God's country.

I made a mental note to ask my daughter when she got home on Sunday if she had been playing with the figurine, but until then I was done racking my brain. I began to make my bed.

But before I finished, I heard a scratching noise, very similar to the noise I had just heard when I moved the lever of the figurine to the off position. Before I could even swallow, the music started playing again.

"Oh, Jesus," I thought to myself. "Grandma, is this you?" I whispered out loud.

I dropped the pillow I had been fluffing and ran to my dresser to see for myself if the lever had actually moved into the on position again . . . and believe it or not, it had.

It was truly an "Oh, my God!" moment. I realized then that Grandma's spirit was just as spunky and determined as she had been in the physical world. Rosie was speaking to me, trying to get me to pay attention to the words of the song: I might have felt as though raindrops were falling on my head, but my life could and *would* get better.

But if you think my hands weren't shaking when I went to pick up that little brass deer the second time, you're wrong. I was shaking like a leaf in a fall breeze. Although I was used to being visited during dreams or readings, this poltergeist-like movement of objects usually didn't happen to me, and it took me off guard. In fact, I was afraid to stay alone in that empty house. I'll admit it; even though I believed that the music going on was a sign from my grandmother, I was chicken and I wanted to run. But, seeing as I wasn't in any shape to run, I thought the best thing would be to call in someone who could confirm that I wasn't losing my mind.

So I phoned my son Chris. I knew he would love to get involved with any paranormal happening. After all, Chris's favorite hobby was ghost busting, or paranormal research. On top of that, Chris and Rosie had been very telepathically connected when she was in the physical realm. If anyone was going to pick up on a sign from her from beyond, it was him. Though I was apprehensive about calling his house so early, I soon realized that if I didn't call someone, my nerves were going to give me an attack. (Stress and anxiety are some of the elements that can cause an MS episode.) So I hesitantly dialed his number. I knew the minute he understood what I was calling about, he'd be excited.

The phone rang twice and Chris picked up. "Mom, are you all right? Is everything okay?" he asked quickly when he answered the phone.

I quickly told him that I was fine and I apologized for calling him so early. Then I hastily clued him in on what had been going on in my bedroom with the musical deer.

Chris was beyond excited. Just the idea that my house could possibly be haunted, or that I was actually receiving physical signs from my grandmother, was like Christmas to him. Before I could get my next sentence out, he said he was coming right over.

Within minutes, Chris was knocking at my door. I opened it and was greeted by my son, armed with a huge grin and a tape recorder.

"Let me see the figurine," he said.

I walked Chris into my bedroom and pointed to the little deer statuette that was sitting silently on my dresser.

"In between the time I hung up with you and your getting

here, it went on again . . . by itself." I was more at ease now with my son there with me.

Chris lifted the little deer in his hand and said, more as a statement than a question, "Can you imagine if it is Grandma Rosie making this thing go on and off?"

"Yes, I can imagine," I said. At that point, I was pretty sure it was her.

Chris set the little statue back down on my dresser, and we waited. But after standing there like statues ourselves for a minute or two, nothing had happened. I decided that I'd make him breakfast while we waited, and we both started to walk out of the bedroom and into my kitchen. Just at the moment our feet hit the kitchen floor, we heard music. But it wasn't the little deer's melody we heard . . . it was another melody from yet another music box.

"La, la, la, la, la, la, la, la . . ." Chris was humming along. "Is that the theme from *The Godfather?*" he asked, laughing even as his face went pale.

"Yeah, I think so," I answered warily. What the hell was going on?

The music that was now playing was coming from my living room, adjacent to the kitchen. Remember earlier I mentioned that I had a collection of music boxes? Well, the one that was playing was a replica of an old-fashioned Victrola. It was given to me for my thirtieth birthday by my old Brooklyn friend LuLu. LuLu said the minute she heard it, she knew she had to buy it for me—she always joked about the major crushes I had on both Al Pacino and Robert De Niro. She figured that since both actors were stars in the *Godfather* movies, the music box would be a most fitting gift for me, and I agreed. I loved that box. It always made me smile, no matter how ill I might have felt that day.

Hearing the music, Chris and I ran into the living room to check it out. This time, I had no doubt there was something paranormal going on. The little deer statuette only had a little lever to move on or off, but this music box had to be wound up to play. And I couldn't for the life of me remember when I had last wound it. My best guess was at least a month or two before.

I now had no doubt that Rosie was behind both music box incidents. Both of the songs from these music boxes held specific messages—answers to the questions I had asked her that morning in my dream. Don't worry if raindrops fall on your head every now and then. The rain will pass. And until it does, get an umbrella. And, as far as the *Godfather* theme song from the other music box . . . well, if you knew Rosie like I knew Rosie, you would understand. My family used to joke about how thankful we were that Grandma was born a woman, because if she had been born a man she probably would have *been* the Godfather. Not because she had the heart of a gangster or was mean or callous, but because she ran her family with respect and loyalty . . . and was tough as nails.

That day was the last day any of my music boxes ever turned on by themselves. (At least for the next four years I lived in that house. It's happened a few more times since then, few and far between.) But the story doesn't end there. Rosie wasn't quite finished sending us signs. This time, it was Chris who saw it first. And to this day, he claims that no paranormal experience will ever beat it.

The night before Rosie's next message, I called Chris to ask him a favor. I had a doctor's appointment the following day, and I knew I might be waiting in the doctor's office for hours. So I asked my son if he'd come over and wait at my house for his sister, just in case I wasn't back when she got home from school at three o'clock. We left it that if I thought I would be late, I'd call him from the doctor's office. Sure enough, at around 2:30 the next day, I gave him a call and told him I still hadn't been seen yet. So he went over to wait for Jackie.

He was at my home in no time, and let himself inside. But when he opened the door to my apartment, he noticed something moving in the darkened living room. Momentarily confused because I had just called him from my doctor's office over twenty miles away, he called out, "Ma, is that you?"

But he got no answer. He ventured inside a little further. My little dog, Sexy, greeted him at the door, so Chris immediately knew it wasn't her shadow on the wall. But as he walked further into the room, he felt a frigid breeze in the corner. He quickly turned on the light and saw what the movement was. It was Rosie's leather rocking chair, something she had given me a long time ago, rocking back and forth by itself. My son, Mister Tough Guy, made a mad dash for the front door. He decided to wait for his sister outside.

When Chris told me about the incident later, I just smiled and said, "Well, Chris, you were always one of her favorites!" And I know, if you asked him today if he was frightened seeing Grandma's chair rocking back and forth, he would say, "No way." But I'll tell you this . . . he's never again gone into my house when no one was home.

Now, I don't believe my late grandmother was haunting my apartment; neither do I believe that she was an unrested soul. What I *do* believe with all my heart and with my sixth sense is that she was trying her hardest to fulfill my wish for a sign. She knew I wanted more than the normal communication I receive when I give a reading. I wanted real validation that Rosie could still hear me.

As usual, Grandma gave much more than she had been asked for.

9.

With Love, from Genni and Joseph

Signs Are Coming Directly to You

As fate and my angels would have it, as I sit down to pen this chapter, the date on my wall calendar reads September 11. As I look outside my window on the West Side of Manhattan, I see that, fittingly enough, the sun has decided to stay inside, as if mimicking the dust, gloom, and darkness of that fateful day not so long ago. My heart is heavy thinking of all the fallen heroes, children, wives, brothers, sisters, mothers, and fathers who were taken from their families and friends, struck down before their time by the evil hands of terrorism. I just want to take a moment to say a prayer and pay my respects not only to the victims' families I have become acquainted with, but also to all the families around the nation. My prayers, and I'm sure the prayers of the world, go out to you this day and every day. May God bless you.

I also want to take a moment on this solemn day to say a prayer for the thousands who were affected by one of the worst natural disasters in American history: those who had to evacuate, those who lost all their possessions, and especially those who passed over. To the victims of Hurricane Katrina, both living and deceased, I send you my prayers and love.

But this chapter isn't meant to be just about fallen heroes or those who have passed over tragically due to nature's fury. This chapter is devoted to all those who have gone into the beyond, whether it be from old age, disease, accident, or natural disaster. This chapter is meant to serve as a voice to let everyone here in the physical domain know that yes, they can hear you when you ask, "Are you okay?" That's the question I'm most often asked in my readings. And you know what my response is? They're not just okay, they're in a joyous, magnificent state of peace and light! A state that few of us here in the physical realm ever allow ourselves to reach. But they—those in spirit—are constantly sending us signs to let us know they're happy, and what's more, that they're watching over us.

I was a psychic medium even before I understood what a "psychic medium" really was. And every time I've communicated with those in spirit, even when I was very young, I've felt an inner tranquility and joy throughout my being. The feeling itself is hard to put into words, but I'll try my best to explain it.

Let's say, for example, it's a Monday morning. By the light shining through my bedroom window and the sound of my daughter's dogs barking in my backyard, I know it's time for me to get up and get started, but I can't for the life of me find the energy or the drive to get going. I've had a very trying weekend: fifteen readings, driving back and forth from Manhattan to Long Island. I'm mentally and physically exhausted. Just the idea of having to get out of bed puts me in a foul mood. But nevertheless, I know I have to get up and begin my day.

Lying there, I go over the day's scheduled readings (I always look at my schedule before I go to sleep) and begin to meditate on them with a few prayers. I ask the spirits to gather around me. As I've said before, my readings don't begin when my phone rings or when a client knocks on my door. My readings begin when I start meditating on whoever is waiting to come through. And as soon as I begin to connect with them, I get a boost of energy that sends my mental antenna into high gear. Suddenly, I find myself in an entirely different state of mind and body than when I first awoke. The grumpy, tired feeling dissipates and is replaced with a sense of peace and joy, not brought on merely by my meditating, but because of my connection with the energies of those waiting to communicate with their loved ones. I know intuitively that we have connected and that our energies have mingled because I start feeling what they are feeling. Remember that in order for me to read them, I have to channel them, and if they were feeling anything but joy, well . . . I would feel that too. When I communicate with an energy that's upset, sad, or just not at peace, my senses make me feel unhappy. That happens a lot when I connect with people in the flesh, in the here and now, so to speak. But whatever the case, as soon as I begin to pick up that kind of energy or mood, I disconnect as quickly as possible. Let me take this chance to remind you: always remember that feelings and attitudes are as catching as the common cold, so make sure you're always in a healthy mental environment. Because when you're in a healthy, happy environment, the energy surrounding you is positive, and it's much easier for you to receive the signs your guides are sending you.

Getting back to my example . . . the positive sense of tranquility begins in my brain and works itself through my entire body. I'm not saying I'm ready to start reading those spirits right away; I'm only trying to get tuned up. I want them to help me find the get-up-and-go and the focus I need, so I ask them to help me recoup my energy. I can only say this: when I commune with positive spirits, it feels as if I've been injected with a B_{12} shot. I'm energized and ready to go. And even more important, my mind is clear and rested and ready to receive the signs they're sending me.

What about you? Is your mind clear and rested? Is the energy around you positive? Are you able to receive signs from your spirit guides?

No? Well, I might be able to help you. If you think you're having trouble receiving signs, here are five simple steps to help you:

1 ♦ *Ask for a sign.* You must make known to the Universe what you want.

2 ♦ *Believe that you'll receive a sign.* Trust that your angels, guides, and loved ones will hear your plea.

3 ♦ *Surrender when you receive a sign . . . remember, no timetables.*

4 ♦ *Always stay calm and peaceful.* When we're excited or anxious, we won't be able to see the sign even if it's hitting us in the face.

5 ♦ *Thank your guides in advance for helping you see the messages they are sending to you.*

And always remember that the signs you do receive aren't just symbolic—they're real ideas that should be incorporated into your life and life journey. The beings who are sending the signs—those in the spiritual domain—are enlightened beyond what our imagination can comprehend. They get their insight from nature and the higher power, and have all received what I like to call a master's degree in teaching. Every day, they're sending us lessons about our destiny in the form of signs. Sometimes those signs are the size of a billboard; other times, they're no bigger than a blade of grass. Sometimes the sign is merely a coincidence. But no matter how big or small it is, it's a sign. This chapter is meant to make you understand that you *can* see and understand the signs you've received all by yourself, without the aid of a psychic medium. Hopefully after reading it, you'll understand that those in spirit are communicating with us constantly, giving us information whether we ask for it or not!

I'm soon going to share with you the stories of two wonderful young people, Giovanna "Genni" Gambale and Joseph Della Pietra, who lost their lives on September 11, 2001. But before I do, let's step back for a moment and observe the synchronicity and timing of the day I started writing this chapter . . . September 11, 2005.

By no means did I ever intend to start this chapter on that day, but as fate and my editor would have it, the book was due. I had been putting off my task because I was having trouble talking about the pain the Gambale and Della Pietra families—the families I'm about to tell you about—had suffered after the World Trade Center tragedy. But when I sat down to write, I suddenly knew: I had no other choice. It was simply the way things were meant to be. I realized that Genni and Joseph had decided to use me as a tool once more. This chapter is a sign, both to me and to their families, that they are still here and feeling our love, and that they have more control now than they ever had.

Of course, we all have free will, and I could certainly have just shut off my computer and waited until the next day to continue—I could have chosen to ignore the sign I was receiving. But I didn't, because there's a huge responsibility that comes with my job. A responsibility to my clients to be honest and caring to all those who seek me out, not only from the physical component of our world, but also from the spiritual. My responsibility lies with them all. After all, isn't that what a psychic medium is supposed to do? Connect with those who have gone beyond? Well, those who have passed over don't just come through when it's convenient for their families and friends; no, they come through anytime they choose, to anyone who is open to receiving the information. They know that I, for one, am ready and willing and open to receive anything they want to express, day or night. No matter what the date happens to be on my calendar. Yes . . . even on this most solemn of days.

Now it's my honor and privilege to share with you two true stories of signs from a loved one that were not only possible, but also miraculous. Let me tell you about the signs sent by Genni and Joseph, the two young people who passed over that infamous day in the World Trade Center.

Genni Gambale and Joseph Della Pietra weren't a romantic couple. Actually, I don't believe they even knew each other while they were here in the physical realm. They may have passed each other in the lobby or on the elevator of the building they worked in, but as far as I know, they never had the opportunity to even say hello. They were like two ships that passed in the night, shrouded from each other by the ocean of the 50,000 other employees who entered the World Trade Center each day. And I'm certain that never for one moment did they believe they would share their final hours together, along with the thousands of others who died that day. But they did. They were struck down in the prime of their lives, leaving behind parents, siblings, and loved ones, and inconsolable grief.

Genni and Joseph were just about the same age, mid- to late twenties. They both were college graduates with very good jobs.

Both came from Italian American families, and both were raised in Brooklyn, New York. They both left behind their parents, a sister and a brother, many relatives and friends, as well as their soul mates. And within a few days of each other, I would get to meet, via the telephone, a member of each one of their families.

The first call I received was from Maryanne Gambale, Genni's mom, a few months after 9/11. Maryanne had heard about me like most people did, through word of mouth. I remember, as though it were yesterday, the first time Maryanne and I spoke. She had never spoken with a psychic before, so she didn't know what to expect from the reading, but she had heard good things about me so she decided to make the call.

To say that Maryanne was in a state of sorrow at the time is much too small a statement to make. The heartache that was enveloping her and her family was beyond words and comprehension. They wanted and needed to know that their daughter's soul and spirit had survived the tragedy, and could still connect with them. They needed Genni to let them know that she had made it over the rainbow and into the arms of angels.

I'll let you judge for yourself . . . but I believe that I was meant to speak with Maryanne. I also believe Genni was the one who set it up. You know how we were talking before about coincidences being signs? Well, what do you think the odds are about these coincidences?

During Maryanne's reading, I received a picture in my head of the parochial school I had gone to, Our Lady of Peace. I immediately told her what I was seeing. (Now, remember I had never spoken with Maryanne before, nor did I know where she lived.) Maryanne informed me that she was a teacher in a school in the Red Hook section of Brooklyn, and that the school she taught in used to be called Our Lady of Peace.

"Okay," I thought, "validations like this aren't uncommon. In fact, they happen all the time." But then I received an image of my godmother Dora. I mentally asked Genni to give me more information on why I was seeing my godmother. Did she just want me to say the name "Dora," in reference to someone from her own family? Or did she want me to acknowledge her own godmother? As I concentrated on receiving the message I realized that she not only wanted me to say the name Dora, but she also wanted me to say my godmother's last name, Novak.

"This woman is going to think I'm nuts," I thought to myself. I mean, what are the odds of someone from my own family playing an integral role in my client's reading? What were the odds of there being two Dora Novaks in New York? These questions mystified me for a few seconds. But I didn't stay baffled for too long, because Genni wasn't backing down. I had to go with what she was showing me no matter what the outcome. So I proceeded to ask Maryanne if the name Dora Novak meant anything to her. It took Maryanne a few seconds to reply, but when she did, her answer blew me away.

"Yes, Mary," she replied. "I know a Dora Novak. Dora worked in the preschool that Genni went to, and Genni loved her."

My first thought was, "Divine intervention," and I felt chills go up and down my spine. But I couldn't let my emotions get in the way of the reading. I wanted to stay in the zone with Genni, so I plowed ahead. I searched my memory and remembered that my godmother Dora did work in a preschool not too far from where Maryanne now worked.

What were the odds of there being two Dora Novaks who worked in a preschool and who lived in the same neighborhood as Maryanne? Astronomical! Coincidence . . . or small miracle? You be the judge.

I told Maryanne that Dora Novak, the lady Genni loved, was in fact my godmother. I cannot put into words the goose bumps I felt when we made that connection. I felt blessed and personally chosen by Genni to help her connect with her mother. You see, I believe that Genni realized that, given her strong Catholic background, her mother would never have called a psychic on her own. In fact, she had more or less always shunned the idea of connecting with anyone who had passed over. But Maryanne said that after she heard about me, her instincts told her that I would understand, and that we could connect with one another. The instinct Maryanne received, I believe, was an emotional whisper from her daughter.

And Genni's whisper was correct—Maryanne and I did connect. And once we did, the connection didn't go away. But I have to be honest: connecting with someone like Maryanne was easy. She's a sweet, lovely woman with a heart as big as the Big Apple itself. Her family is her life force, and the energy running through her (and the rest of them) is so immense and full of love that it runs like a perfectly timed Swiss clock. When I connected with Genni, she showed me that she felt blessed to be a part of such a wonderful family, and that she couldn't have asked for anything more.

By the time my reading with Maryanne ended, I knew Genni's energy would be commuting between her family and me for a while, and that was fine with me. Before hanging up I told Maryanne to watch for signs from her daughter, and she promised she would.

A few months had passed since my call with Maryanne when Genni's sister Antoinette scheduled a reading. During our reading, I received a mental picture of flowers—if I recall correctly, I believe the flowers Genni kept showing me were lavender or blue. At the time, neither Antoinette nor I could say what the flowers meant. But when things like that happen—when the signs we get just don't seem to make sense at the moment—I tell all my clients to write the information down and save it for later. Antoinette did. As I continued with the reading, Genni kept showing me pictures of flowers. I intuitively knew that for her to keep showing me the same sign meant the flowers were very special to her. I couldn't make out the meaning just yet, but I knew in time it would become clear.

One month later, I received a call from Antoinette saying that the family had received another message from Genni. This time, there was no way it could have been mistaken for a figment of someone's imagination or any kind of coincidence.

Antoinette had been in the backyard of the family's summer house on Long Island when she passed a hydrangea bush (commonly known as a "snowball bush," from the ball shape of the flower heads) that had been there for years. The blossoms of the flowers were a lavender-blue. After taking a moment to reflect on their color, Antoinette was about to walk away when she saw something odd—a blossom ball shaped exactly like a valentine heart. She ran into the house to get her mother to come out and see. When she arrived, Maryanne couldn't believe her eyes. There was no mistaking it: it was a perfectly shaped heart, about five inches across and five inches in height. Antoinette ran back into the house to get her camera to take a picture. Now, we all know that the camera doesn't lie—it doesn't produce anything on film that is a figment of someone's imagination. The photo that Antoinette took shows a beautiful hydrangea flower head shaped exactly like a valentine heart. As soon as the film was developed, Maryanne had copies made and then made the photos into bookmarks with a little note that read, *With Love from Genni!*

Maryanne sent me a bookmark as well as a larger photo, which I keep in a frame on my desk. I keep the bookmark in my wallet so I can look at Genni's miracle every day. There is no doubt in my mind that Genni's energy created the gift for her family and friends to show her love and appreciation for their prayers and undying love. The flowering heart was also the answer that her family needed, the validation that Genni had reached the arms of the angels. Believe me, miracles like that need heaven's help.

As I gave more and more readings to her family in the coming months, Genni always showed me her good nature and great sense of humor by letting me know whenever someone was about to call who was connected to her in some way. "Boy, I sure get a lot of company," was the expression that would pop into my mind, as I meditated before my next reading. Whenever I heard that phrase, I was sure that whomever I was scheduled to read next was connected with Genni in some way. That was Genni's sign to me, her calling card. After all, that's really what signs actually are . . . calling cards or announcements from the spiritual realm.

Of course, some of you may believe that my knowledge that a person calling me would be connected to Genni is just a coincidence. For those of you who do, let me just clue you in to how many requests I get for readings in a day. It could be anywhere from ten to two hundred. Either way, the odds of me knowing that my next scheduled reading would somehow be someone connected to that young woman are astronomically high, about as good as finding a needle in a haystack. I'm not a magician, I'm a psychic. And a psychic is only as good as the energy she is reading. Genni's energy is always clear and static-free.

Genni, I know you can hear me. I want you to know that this chapter is for your family. It's for Joseph's family. And it's for the two of you.

As he was in the physical world, Joseph Della Pietra is a gentleman in spirit. He wanted Genni's story to go first. Joseph, we thank you for your patience. But now it's your turn. . . .

I met Joseph the same way I met Genni: through his mother. Like Maryanne Gambale, Sandra Della Pietra found me through word of mouth. Like Maryanne, Sandra had never before had a psychic reading, and was hesitant to have one. But also like Maryanne, she was having trouble coming to terms with the loss of her child, and needed to talk to someone. She called me right around the same time as Maryanne, maybe just within a few days of her. She was, to say the least, heartbroken as well as in a state of utter disbelief and shock. Her son Joseph, her baby boy, the last of her three children, had perished in the towers. They had been closer than close, and she was very proud of everything he had accomplished in life, including his recent graduation from Columbia University.

Though he made light of his abilities, Joseph was extraordinarily intelligent. But he also loved to have a good time with his friends. On our first reading, Joseph came through and gave me scenic mental pictures of what looked very much like Mexico. When I informed Sandra what Joseph was showing me, she told me that their last vacation together was in Mexico. During the same reading, Joseph gave me the names of both his siblings and made me feel the closeness and love he felt for them. He also gave me images of things he loved to do, and showed me the school he had graduated from (Columbia). He acknowledged a scholarship in his name that he seemed very proud of. He acknowledged the car he drove, and also gave me information for others in his family, as well as for his girlfriend.

But what I recall the most from my first reading with Sandra was Joseph's acknowledgment of his sister Lisa. It's not unusual for those in spirit to give me the names of their siblings, but this was different. Even after our session was over, Joseph kept whispering her name in my head: "Lisa . . . Lisa . . . Lisa." You know when you can't get a song you've heard on the radio out of your head? Well, that's the way it was with Lisa's name. I knew that Joseph was trying to tell me that Lisa was still in his thoughts, and that he was trying very hard to communicate with her. He wanted his sister to know that he was okay.

Before we ended our session, Sandra said she would try to have her daughter call me, but she also told me she wasn't sure if Lisa was ready to do so. I told Sandra not to push her daughter into having a reading, but just to pass along the information she received in hers, which Sandra did.

Thankfully, after a while, the thoughts of Lisa left me, and I was able to continue with my daily routine. But then, a few days later, while I was on the phone with a friend, I heard her name whispered in my ear over and over again. "Okay," I said out loud while still holding the receiver in my hand, "I know it's you, Joey, but what do you want me to do?"

"Who are you talking to?" asked my friend Lynne.

"I'm talking to a young man named Joseph who I read the other day."

"How do you mean, you read him the other day? Do you mean you read *him* or you read his *family*?" she asked, perplexed.

"I read his mother, but he's the one talking to me. I know it."

I was sure it was Joseph. For some reason, he had started whispering "Lisa" again. After a few minutes, the whispering ceased, and Lynne and I continued our conversation. But moments later, we were interrupted by the beep of call waiting on my phone. Without looking at my caller ID, I blurted out to Lynne, "This must be Lisa on the line."

"What makes you think that?" she asked. "Has her name popped up on the caller ID?"

"No, it just says 'Out of Area,' but I know it's her."

"How?" she asked.

"Because Joseph announced her in my head before she called. Hold on while I make sure it's her." I clicked the line once. And before anyone said a word, Joseph made me feel I was supposed to say these exact words to the caller: "Hello, is this Lisa?"

There was complete and utter silence on the other end, so I said it again. "Hello, is this Lisa?"

"Yes, this is Lisa," said a very shaky female voice.

"Don't worry, Lisa," I said, feeling her alarmed energy. "Joseph made me feel you were about to call. I couldn't get your name out of my head."

I realized after I spoke with her that Joseph needed to give his sister an extreme sign that he was still with her. She was grieving so badly for him, she couldn't see the signs that he had been sending her and her family on his own. And believe me, there were plenty of them . . . like a good prankster, sometimes Joseph played tricks on his mother by making her TV go on and off. And once, Sandra told me she heard footsteps in the house when no one else was home. But most of all, she always felt the energy of his love and good nature, especially on the grimmest days. I knew now that Lisa could feel it too.

Of late, Joseph has begun connecting with another female family member: his two-year-old niece Grace. Sandra and I recently had a conversation, and she shared this remarkable story with me. I've entitled it "The Locket."

It seems about six months ago, Sandra's young granddaughter, who is loquacious for her age, pointed to the gold locket around her grandmother's neck that held a picture of her late son and asked, "Nana, who's that?"

Sandra replied to little Grace, who never had the privilege of meeting her uncle, "It's your uncle Joseph, your daddy's brother. Someday I'll tell you all about him."

Little Grace answered back, "I want to see him, Nana."

With tears choking her throat, Sandra said, "Uncle Joseph's in heaven and someday I'll tell you all about him." She left it at that. After all, Grace was only two, much too young to understand why she couldn't meet her uncle.

Six months later, Sandra was at the house of her oldest son Carl—Grace's dad—for dinner. As they were enjoying a family dinner in the dining room, out of nowhere little Grace announced that she wanted to go home with Nana Sandra and sleep over at her house. Sandra replied to her granddaughter, "Are you sure you want to come with me? You know I live a long way from Mommy and Daddy's house, and I can't drive you home in the middle of the night."

Little precocious Grace immediately answered, "Absolutely!"

Everyone at the table laughed at how smart and articulate little Grace had become, but Grace wasn't through. She added, "Nana, I have to come . . . Uncle Joseph wants me there!"

The family stood in awe of what they had just heard. Little Grace, who had never met her uncle Joseph, her daddy's brother, seemed to have been communicating with him on her own. And from what I've heard from Sandra, there are times when Grace is talking in her room. When she's asked who she's speaking to, she confidently replies, "Uncle Joseph."

So whether you ask for signs or not, they'll arrive via Heaven Express . . . with love, from your angels.

Genni and Joseph, you love your families so much. You have taught everyone you ever touched in this world, and also the next, that love is eternal. And the lesson we should all learn is this: when you least expect it, you'll receive a sign of love to let you know there is much more to the Universe than you ever imagined. We've only just begun to become enlightened by our spirit guides, to really be able to read the signs we receive. Heck, even I'm still learning! But the important thing is to keep your heart and mind open to the kinds of signs Genni and Joseph sent. To the kinds of signs we get every day. To the kind of signs like the one that prompted me to write this book: the dove.

And what better way for me to close this chapter for Genni, Joseph, and myself than to bid you all the Sign of the Dove, the sign of peace, which is the best sign of all.

I bid you peace and I wish you eternal love.

And remember, it's okay for us to expect miracles because when we do, we're sure to receive them.

I'm expecting. Won't you join me?

10.

Atlantic City

You Always Come Out a Winner . . .
When You Listen to Your Angels and Guides

In this chapter, I want to talk about the concept of free will. Whether or not you choose to acknowledge and follow the directions being sent to you by your angels and guides is entirely up to you. But I believe that spiritual guidance is something we all should accept freely because there are lessons for us to learn, and our guides are pointing us in the right direction. After all, the main reason why we experience anything in life, either good or bad, is for the lessons those experiences provide. So we might as well take the path that will do us the most good. But even though accepting guidance is all up to us, there are times when our angels will be so adamant about something that they'll keep hitting us over the head with signs until we finally get it. And I'm not against a little shove from time to time in the right direction. In fact, I believe those little shoves, jolts, and pushes are the main reason we have guides in the first place. Guiding us is their job.

What? You didn't know that your guides and angels had jobs in heaven? Well, what do you think they do up there . . . sit back on a cloud and eat bonbons with Gandhi and Moses? Nah, I don't think so. In fact, I think Gandhi and Moses are working too. Truth be told, I believe it was a psychic medium who came up with the phrase "Life's a bitch and then you die." Because he or she knew you never stop working, even after you've passed over. (All jokes aside, I don't know who actually came up with that phrase, but I just had to throw it in here. My grandmother made me do it!)

But seriously speaking, we never stop working and helping others. Actually, we're *supposed* to be helping others much more while we're here on earth so once we get to the next plane, helping people—acting as spiritual guides—is second nature to us.

At this point, you might be wondering who your angels and guides are (and yes, we all have them). It may be a loved one who has crossed over or a neighbor who used to live next door. A guide can also be someone you've never known, but who went through many similar life experiences and now has wisdom they want to share with you. I've even received guidance from the people I have read. Our guides, and most of us have many, are always watching out for us and helping us. If you've been paying attention at all so far to this book, you'll have figured out that the signs your guides send can be helpful to you in every aspect of your life, whether it's a relationship, medical information, or just a major decision. If we would just pay attention to those signs and listen to our instincts, our lives would be so much easier. And isn't that what we're all searching for, a way to make our lives easier?

It was two of my own guides (introduced to me by readings I had with their family members) who taught me the lesson that when we cross over, our jobs don't end. In fact, they have only just begun. . . .

It was March 2002 when my aunt Margaret called to say she had complimentary rooms at Bally's Hotel and Casino in Atlantic City, and to ask if I'd like to go with her. Aunt Margaret and I had been AC (Atlantic City) buddies forever—sometimes we'd take the bus there as often as once a month, or we'd drive the almost two hundred miles from Long Island. Aunt Margaret knew how much I loved Atlantic City and playing the slots. She was also well aware I hadn't been able to go there for the last two years because of the progression of my illness. But although she was very familiar with my medical circumstances, she somehow felt that the offer was a sign that we were meant to go. Feelings and intuition run like water in my family, and my aunt Margaret was following hers. Aunt Margaret sensed I needed a break from my readings, which since September 11, I had been giving nonstop, seven days a week. You see, at that time I was finding it very hard to disconnect from my readings after they were done. I realized that not only was I becoming emotionally attached to those in the spirit realm, but also to their families. Which meant that, even after the readings were over, I worried about them as I would my own family. I didn't know what to do with all the emotion and sorrow I felt for the victims' families, and Aunt Margaret felt a trip to Atlantic City would be just what the doctor ordered.

When she first told me about the free room offer at one of my favorite casinos, I got that old excited feeling again, and recalled all the good times we'd had in the past, sitting side by side at adjacent slot machines throwing coins in until our fingers were black. But I told my aunt that I had to think about it. I wanted to go, but at that moment I didn't think it was a good idea—I just didn't know if my condition would allow it.

That night, as I lay in bed, I rethought my aunt's offer. I had to admit I missed hearing the ching, ching, ching of the money falling down from the slot machines. So I started trying to come up with a plan that would allow me to take this trip. The main reason I didn't want to go was the way I felt last time we went, when I did the driving, so I immediately eliminated that possibility. But I also knew my aunt wouldn't be able to drive either because of an injury to her shoulder she'd received in a car accident years before. So if we were to go, we'd need a third person. But it couldn't be just any person—it would have to be someone I felt confident and secure with, and who was willing to drive the four-hours to AC. And, of course, who enjoyed the casinos as much as we did.

As far as I was concerned, there was only one person who fit all the criteria: my son Christopher. The next morning, just on a whim, I brought up my aunt's invitation to Chris. At the time my son was living in an apartment downstairs from me, and we would see each other each morning in passing. We were just making small talk when I informed him about Aunt Margaret's comped room at the casino. I told him that I had more or less scratched the idea of going . . . I didn't have to elaborate on the reasons why because Chris knew. Much to my surprise, Chris responded with optimistic confidence and said he would love to drive us. He said that he really didn't care whether or not he gambled, he just wanted to help me get out a little in any way he could. Chris wasn't wearing blinders with regard to my physical limitations—he knew all too well just what my restrictions were. But my son also believed I was getting better since I began using my positive visualization tapes and started a new diet, both of which I had implemented since the last time I went to Atlantic City.

"But Chris," I said, "what about walking on the casino floor? You know and I know I can't walk that distance from the parking lot to the hotel." But I continued, "I guess I could just rent one of those scooters." I was trying to give myself more options.

"Maybe you won't have to," he said. "We'll just make sure you don't have to do a lot of walking. And maybe this is an opportunity for you to start venturing out again and seeing what you can and can't do."

Although I was already quite sure I knew what I could and could not do, I desperately wanted the opportunity to get back some semblance of the life I once knew. Chris was right—I needed to at least try. Who knew, maybe I would have a great time. After all, I was still the same Mary who loved staying in hotels and taking long car rides (as I had before my illness had progressed).

So I decided to do what I tell everyone else to do when they're unsure of a decision they have—I surrendered!

With Aunt Margaret and Chris confident that I should go, I began leaning that way too. After speaking with my son, I immediately called my aunt and told her I would take her up on her offer, and that Chris had just volunteered to drive us. Aunt Margaret was thrilled, to say the least, and asked me to call and make the reservations for us when I knew what my schedule looked like.

You didn't need to be psychic to know that Christopher was the perfect person to accompany Aunt Margaret and me. One, he loved AC just as much as we did. Two, he understood my condition better than anyone else, having shared the same house with me. Oh, and let's not forget that he was my son! And no one knows us better than our own children . . . no one. My son and I more or less grew up with each other. As I stated before, I was only eighteen when Chris was born, and sometimes I felt more like his sister than his mother. No, there was no person more perfect to go with us than Christopher.

"But what am I going to do about exhaustion?" I asked myself silently. At that point, I hadn't found anything that helped me feel more energetic. (This was just a few months before I found the medication that would change my life, Prokarin, a transdermal cream developed by Elaine DeLack.) At the time I still felt wiped out most of the time, so much that I had to drive my car to my mailbox thirty feet away from my front door. The only way I could think of to save energy was to not give readings at least a day before we went, because readings always exhausted me.

Without delay, I began to check my schedule to find out what date would be the best for me to go. Although I was locked inside my four walls because of my physical limitations, I was still giving phone readings seven days a week, so I had to see when I could squeeze in some downtime. I saw that I had a few free days in the middle of March. I decided on Thursday, the fifteenth, figuring I could take my weekly interferon injection right before we left. (I didn't want to leave on the same day as my injection, because the side effects you get within the first twenty-four hours can include fever and aches and pains. But the comped room was only for a Thursday or Friday night so I had no other choice.)

I circled the fifteenth on my calendar. I can honestly say I wasn't all that excited about going. Realistically, I knew I wouldn't be able to do much while I was there. But I no longer considered our trip to AC to be a minivacation—it had become my mission. I knew I was being directed there, and I just had to trust in the Universe and follow the signs that were coming my way.

The departure day came quickly. Chris came home from work early, and by 4 P.M. both he and Aunt Margaret were waiting for me to take my injection. Right before we took off, I asked my son if he could check the mailbox. (I didn't want to leave mail in my mailbox overnight.) Chris retrieved a pile of mail for me. I was about to drop the stack on the kitchen table, to be opened up when I got back, when I saw a familiar name on an envelope—it was a letter from Pat Murphy, one of my dear clients who lost her nephew Brian, a firefighter, on September 11: (These names have been changed to protect the privacy of the people involved.) I put the rest of the mail on the table and took a second to read Pat's letter.

Dear Mary,

I think about you so very often and remember our first reading when my nephew Brian came through. And since then, I've realized there were just too many coincidences after his passing that led us to each other, so I thought you'd like to see what Brian looked like when he was here. Enclosed is his mass card with his picture. Keep him with you as an additional guardian angel because I know he's looking down at us and guiding us because as you mentioned in our session, "That's just the way he was."

Again, I just felt this urge to write you and send you Brian's picture. Take care and speak to you again soon.

Love,
Pat

"Okay," I said out loud, looking down at Brian's handsome face on his mass card, "I guess you want to come with me." I put Brian's photo into my bag and locked my front door. I walked toward the car where my aunt and son were patiently waiting. As I opened the door to take a seat, I said, "Now I'm sure we're supposed to go to Atlantic City today because I just received a letter from heaven telling me it's okay to go."

"What letter?" asked my son.

"This letter," I said as I reached into my handbag to retrieve Pat's letter and Brian's mass card.

"For some reason," I continued, "I believe Brian wants me to go to AC, and I don't believe it has anything to do with my winning at the slots. I actually think I'm supposed to go because of something he wants me to see, or something he wants me to sense. I also think he's telling me I have to get used to going out again, even if I have to stay in the hotel room the entire time we're there. And—I know this is going to sound crazy to you—I actually think I'm going to be receiving some kind of sign from him and Robert Curatola when we get there."

"Now you've totally lost me," answered Chris.

"I'm lost too," my aunt chimed in.

"I get why you think Brian is telling you it's okay to go to AC, but what does Robert Curatola have to do with anything?" asked Chris curiously.

Before I answered, I opened my wallet and pulled out another mass card. It was Robert's, and I had received it in the mail months earlier from his wife Christine. Robert Curatola was another young firefighter who passed over on that infamous day. He and his family had been some of the people I couldn't let go of after my readings. Robert, in turn, had become a guardian angel to me and to my daughter Jackie. I wrote about him in my first book, *Beyond These Four Walls*, in a chapter entitled "Someone to Watch Over Me."

I continued explaining, "Robert's is the only other mass card I thought to bring with me today. I brought it because I wanted his help with courage for this trip. And it's funny, because I've become close with both Robert's and Brian's families. Both these young men are on my mind all the time, and one of the reasons I agreed

I needed to get away from the house was to take my mind off all the questions I ask myself about these two young firefighters."

"What kind of questions?" asked my son, as he pulled out of the driveway.

"Questions to the Universe and to those two boys. I ask for a sign that my interpretation of what they're trying to say to me is correct. I also ask them to show me how they were feeling before they passed."

"Why would you need them to show you a sign?" asked Chris. "Didn't you get all the signs you needed when you read their families?"

"Yes, of course I received signs, but most of the time I feel those signs are for their loved ones. When I'm by myself and meditating, I ask them for a sign to me, as their friend and not as their interpreter.

"You know," I continued, "I don't think any medium is totally equipped to handle all the emotions that go along with the job. Sometimes, no matter how long you've been doing it or how good you are at receiving information, you just need reassurance that you're doing the right thing by everyone, yourself included."

Chris and Margaret both acknowledged that they understood what I meant. We pulled onto the Long Island Expressway, heading west, and began our drive to Atlantic City.

As Chris drove, we made small talk about everything going on in each other's lives, and then once again our conversation turned toward the Universe and life after life. As our discussion continued, I asked my son and aunt if they wanted to hear an audiotape I had brought along with me for the ride. I had brought my own headset and tape player, but I realized since we were talking about the Universe and the energy of life anyway, they might enjoy listening to one of my favorite tapes by Deepak Chopra, where he speaks about the laws of the Universe. Chris and Margaret said they'd love to hear it, and Chris popped it into the car's tape player. We listened and commented that we were in total agreement with what Dr. Chopra was saying: that the Universe has a life and mind of its own, that it speaks to us, and that all we have to do to get a response back is to tell the Universe what our true intentions are.

As we listened, we interjected here and there about certain laws he was speaking about. I commented that I believed he was right on target with his teachings, but that he could only give us the equation to life. As students of life, we had to figure out and believe in our intentions with all our hearts. If we didn't mean what we intended, we shouldn't bother to ask for anything, or to expect an answer. I also added that we all think we understand what we have to do in order to get the results we're looking for, but sometimes we give up too soon—like I had almost done with this trip. I said that I believed that this small journey to Atlantic City might actually be a turning point for me, and could possibly answer a lot of my questions.

I thanked my aunt Margaret and Chris again for being my earth angels in helping me find myself. I also thanked them for giving me the extra courage and security I needed for this trip.

I know you may be thinking, "Geez, she was only going to Atlantic City, not Europe, so what's the big deal?" But to me it might as well have been Europe, because this was the farthest journey I had taken in over two years. In fact, in recent months I couldn't remember being in a car for more than ten minutes at a time—I just wasn't feeling well enough. So for me, getting in a car with the intention of taking a four-hour drive and staying in a hotel overnight was *huge*. I had every intention of telling the Universe that I was serious about my desire to be better. But I'm not going to lie and say I wasn't nervous, because I was. I was sweating bullets inside. But I felt I had no other choice. I wanted to live, not just exist in a shell of a life. And in order to do so, I needed answers about my own capabilities. Thank God my family was there for me to give me that extra boost I needed to truly surrender.

A little after 8 P.M., we pulled into Bally's parking garage. The ride itself wasn't too bad. In fact, I held up pretty well, but I was really tired. I was praying that I had the strength to walk into the casino and check in. If I could just do that, I prayed silently to the Man up above, I'd be very, very happy. I would have felt this trip was already a complete success.

Chris parked the car, but before we began our trek into the casino, I stood by the car door, trying to measure with my eyes just how long a walk it was from the car to the garage elevator. My estimation was about forty feet. Then I mentally calculated the walk from the elevator to the escalator (which was easy for me; I knew the casino like the back of my hand, having been there so often in the past with my aunt). That was the walk that really scared me.

I know what you're thinking. "Why the heck didn't she just get into a wheelchair and save herself all the anxiety?" Why? Because I knew in my heart I wasn't supposed to. I knew deep down if I could make this walk, there was hope for me someday down the line. Like I said before, I was on a mission, and this short jaunt to Atlantic City could answer many questions.

As I stood frozen by my car door, I looked at my son for reassurance with tears in my eyes.

"Chris, I can do this, right?"

Chris looked back at me with the same glance I remembered him giving me when he was a little boy of eleven, as he was being wheeled into an operating room to have major surgery. As his nurse and I walked beside his gurney on the long walk toward the operating room, the nurse commented how secure and calm he seemed. The nurse looked down at my son as he lay on his portable bed and told him how proud she was of him, because he had shown more composure and courage before his operation than some adults. As we continued walking, the nurse informed my son that if he was worried about anything, he should tell her his concerns and she would explain the procedure to him. But my brave little soldier answered her with a statement that shocked even me.

Looking straight at me, he asked, "Are you afraid, Mom?"

Startled by his question, I answered spontaneously, "No, Chris, I'm not afraid. You'll be just fine."

"Then I'm not afraid," stated my son, this time looking directly at his nurse.

The nurse looked at both of us and said, "Well, you must have a lot of confidence in your mother."

"I do," said my son, as he looked into my eyes for any signs of fear I might have hidden. As Chris continued to look into my soul, he added, "If my mother's not afraid, then I'm not afraid."

With that said, the nurse wheeled his gurney into the operating room and I went into the waiting room, choking back my tears and (of course) my parental fears. But before the nurse departed she said, "I've been a pediatric nurse for over fifteen years and I've come to understand that children pick up the energy of their parents. If the parents are confident, then they are too, so keep up the good work, mom."

That was the first life lesson that proved to me that we are the mirror of our environment, and I have never forgotten it.

Now the tides were turned and I was the one looking into my son's eyes for confidence, just the way he had looked into mine so many years before. I'm happy to say that I found the extra strength I needed in my son's eyes and in his tone. He looked at me and said, "Mom, you've come this far. I'm so proud of you for trying, and I know you can make it the rest of the way."

Suddenly, I knew I could do it. If Chris wasn't frightened for me, then neither was I. My son's eyes gave me the power and the courage to walk the longest I had to walk in two years. Slowly but surely, I made it to the escalator. Tired and achy—but I made it all the same.

However, I wasn't about to get overconfident. As we rode up the escalator to the front desk, I told my aunt that we should inform the clerk that I was disabled and that I would require, if it was available, a room on the lowest floor possible, just in case.

"Just in case of what?" asked my aunt, a little startled by my request. (I sometimes forget that, as a psychic, I can't just say things without people fearing the reason behind my comments.)

"Just in case we have to evacuate," I answered.

"Evacuate! Why would we have to evacuate? You don't see anything bad happening, do you?" she asked, more than a little frightened as to what I might be sensing.

"Don't worry," I said. "I don't foresee any major problems, but this is the first time I've been in a big building in years. Since the World Trade Center tragedy, I'd feel much better being able to walk down the stairs if for some reason we needed to leave suddenly. And if we're up on the higher floors, I don't think I'd be able to climb down all the way without needing help."

We got to the front desk and I stood beside my aunt as she showed them her identification and her invitation for a complimentary room. Just before they were going to give her a room number, she made the request for a room on a lower level to accommodate me. The very personable young man at the desk was extremely kind and gave us a room on the same floor as the casino—just a few feet away from the desk we were standing at. Another small miracle, and another positive sign that we were in the right place at the right time. Everything was falling into place, and I was ecstatic.

I couldn't wait to put my overnight bag down and just sit and rest for a moment. I was exhausted from the long walk from the parking garage and, thanks to the interferon injection, I was feeling feverish and achy. Chris and Aunt Margaret were also tired from the long ride, and wanted to wash up and rest a while too before they ventured onto the casino floor to gamble.

About a half hour later, we were all ready to make a killing at the slots. Margaret reported she had found three open machines neighboring each other. Although pooped, I was happy about the idea of playing my first coins in two years, and thrilled to once again hear the sweet sound of the slot machine.

There was only one little snag. When I turned the corner of the corridor onto the casino floor, I came face-to-face with my archenemy . . . the red rug.

There it was again, living and breathing with a life of its own, the speckled scarlet carpet taunting me. You see, two years earlier, its intricate pattern tortured my nervous system and put me completely off balance. I couldn't stay in the room for very long without getting ill. But this time, I made myself look down at it, testing my ability to withstand it. I needed to see if its multicolored spots still affected me the same way they had before. They didn't. And even more than that, I felt this rug could never beat me, because I had already won the jackpot. I had made it back to Atlantic City. With the help of my family, the Mary I had once known was fighting her way back, one quarter at a time. I was in no rush and would just take one step at a time, one trip at a time, and one sign at a time, finding my way back to a healthy and better me.

I lasted at the slots almost an entire hour before I felt the need to retire to our room. I knew my son couldn't really enjoy himself while watching my every move the way he had been doing. Although he had confidence in me, he knew all too well how much this outing had taken out of me, and how long it had been since I had attempted doing so much in one day. So, I bid my aunt Margaret and son good night, and walked back to our room alone.

When I got back, I changed into a jogging suit and put on the television just in time to watch *ER*, one of my favorite Thursday night shows. It was just 10 P.M. and although my body was physically exhausted from our excursion, I was nevertheless restless. I suspected it was because of my injection—I always found it hard to sleep the first night after the shot.

I watched the entire episode of *ER*. After it was over, I channel-surfed for a while, seeing if there was anything else worthwhile on the boob tube. Finding nothing that interested me, I shut off the TV and went into my overnight bag and pulled out my portable tape player and headset. I've always found that listening to either an audiobook or meditation tape relaxes me enough to doze off when I'm having one of my insomniac nights. So I popped in a meditation tape I'd brought along.

No luck . . . after about a half hour of listening to the tape, I was still wide awake.

I lay there in bed, looking up at the darkened ceiling and deliberating. I thought about all the things we had accomplished this day, and about the synchronicity of events that had transpired to bring us here. But then, out of nowhere, my mind started running away with itself—I started asking myself all kinds of what-ifs. Our hotel was a huge building—what if we were attacked the way the World Trade Center was? What would I do, and how would I react? What if there was a fire? Would I be calm or hysterical?

From the first what-if, I knew I was in the initial stages of a panic attack. I immediately began reasoning with myself the only way I knew how—talking to Robert and Brian, my firefighter angels, in my head. I asked them to help me calm myself. I asked them to please help me get over my fears and anxieties, especially about being so far away from home. And most of all, I asked them to help make me sure, once and for all, they were truly okay, and that it wasn't just me who could hear them, but that they could hear me too.

I knew without a doubt that I had connected with them on many occasions before, but I had never asked them to communicate solely with me. And you know what? They did. After a few minutes, the panic began to dissipate. I still wasn't able to fall asleep, but at least I wasn't panicking. Just speaking with them calmed me. But, seeing that I was still awake, I decided to say a few prayers to help me keep my cool. I was still praying at 2:30 A.M., when my aunt Margaret found her way to our room, dog tired and ready for sleep.

We spoke a little while before she conked out, and she told me she had more or less come out even on the slots. But the minute her head hit the pillow, she fell asleep. I was so envious of her gift of slumber, I could have screamed! But I just lay there with my rosary beads in my hands, praying for just a couple of stinking winks.

My prayers must have been working because just a few minutes later, around 3 A.M., I finally felt myself drift off to sleep. But then at around 3:30 I was awakened by the sound of our hotel room door opening again. It was Chris coming in from his night at the slots. We spoke for a brief second; he said he was up a few bucks, but then he threw himself on his bed. Within seconds, he was snoring away. Yep, you guessed it . . . I was still awake praying.

Having pretty much given up on sleep, I decided to read for a while. I got up from my bed and went back into my overnight bag and pulled out a paperback novel. Not to disturb the two sleeping beauties, I then grabbed one of the chairs from the bedroom and dragged it quietly into the extraordinarily large bathroom (it was a wheelchair-accessible room). I turned on the bathroom light, shut the door, and began to read. No more than five or ten minutes later, the red alarm lights on the wall of the bathroom began to flicker on and off. These were the lights used for the hearing impaired, to tell them if there was a fire emergency in the building.

At first my brain didn't comprehend what I was seeing. But then it hit me—this was a real emergency! I immediately opened the bathroom door to see that the other lights by the nightstand were also going on and off. Suddenly, I heard a voice coming over the loudspeaker in the hallway saying, "This is not a drill, this is a fire emergency. All occupants are to evacuate their rooms immediately!"

"Dear God," I thought. "Is this really happening, or have I finally fallen asleep? Am I having a nightmare?"

I mentally fired off questions to Brian and Robert. "Was this why I was panicking this evening? Were you guys warning me of this?"

Now I knew why, as soon as I got off the escalator, I had had the sense of urgency to ask for a room close to the street. I had been directed from my friends in spirit, Robert and Brian. I no longer had any doubt that not only could they hear me—I knew they also could communicate with me in a big way.

Believe it or not, with all this going on, my son and my aunt were still sound asleep. I know that both my firefighter angels would have been proud of me, because I very calmly and swiftly woke each one of them. I told them to get their shoes on and leave everything else behind except any medications.

Within seconds, we were out of the room and in the corridor. I found myself knocking on other occupants' hotel doors, telling them to get up and out. Within minutes our entire floor—the floor designated for people with disabilities—was evacuated. We were told to wait in the front lobby by the casino while the hotel security checked out the reason why the fire alarm had gone off.

But I didn't need anyone from the hotel to tell me what had occurred. I already knew. It was Robert and Brian speaking to me the only way they could. They had given me the hugest sign they could muster—making the fire alarm go off so I could see how I would have reacted in such a case. And that was with calm assurance and logic. In fact, my son commented later that I, the one with the disability and the one who had the most fears about coming to Atlantic City, was the calmest person on the floor. And you know what? . . . I was. But I had help. I had the help of my two firefighter buddies, who I now had no doubt could speak to me directly.

After fifteen or twenty minutes of standing in the lobby, we were told it was safe to go back into our rooms. The fire alarm had to do with them recently painting the floor directly below ours—something about the sprinkler system being covered. After the hotel security guard finished with his explanation, I asked him if this was a normal occurrence in the hotel. His response was, "Absolutely not. In fact," he continued, "this is the first time it's ever gone off on my shift, and I've been here for years."

Was our experience in Atlantic City a mere coincidence or a sign? You judge for yourself. You have free will to believe whatever you choose. As for my family and me . . . well, let's just say we never leave home without Robert's or Brian's mass cards. Just remember this: whether you're aware of it or not, your angels and guides are always watching you, trying to alleviate your fears, and helping you win at the game of life.

11.

Recognize the Signs

Learning to Trust Your Intuition

One of the very first questions I'm usually asked when I tell a client to watch for signs is "How will I know if something is an actual sign?" It's a good question. If the phone rings and no one is there when you pick it up, is it dear departed Uncle John telling you he has made it to the Other Side, or is it just a wrong number? If your lights flicker or pop when you turn on a lamp, is it a sign that you have a spirit visitor or does it mean you have electrical problems? As I said before, I don't believe in coincidences, but I also don't go around thinking that everything that happens on a day-to-day basis has some hidden or supernatural meaning. That would drive anyone crazy. And besides, it's not true. Sometimes things just happen because they happen. Not coincidentally, but because of normal everyday wear and tear.

So how can you tell the natural from the supernatural? Well, let's say that you've been praying for some kind of sign from a loved one who has passed over, and you feel frustrated because you haven't recognized any and in desperation you say something like, "If you can hear me, can you send me a sign now, please?" And suddenly your phone rings and you answer it but no one's on the other end. Is that a sign? Sometimes . . . but they can send you more, much more. Spirit energy can also create static on the line that sometimes gets louder and louder every time you say hello. This type of occurrence is more common than most people realize. But again, they can and do send more intricate signs by use of the telephone. How do I know? Well, I've trained myself to be sort of a psychic detective, checking the facts and the evidence of a sign to determine how complex it is. And believe me, the signs we receive just by use of the telephone can be intricate but not difficult for you to determine. Usually a sign is multifaceted. For example, often what's happening when the phone rings and there's no one on the other end is that our guides are giving us messages even through caller ID. Most of the time when that happens, there is also no name on the caller ID (or it says NO DATA SENT). Other times, the same sign plays out differently—let's say there is a name on the caller ID, even though there's no one on the line. Well, what I usually find is that there's some additional common thread between the person's name listed on caller ID and the person you were hoping to receive a sign from. For example, let's say you're hoping to hear from Grandma Maria; the name on the caller ID could be Maria, Marie, or Grandma Maria's husband's or child's name. They'll always try to use a name that has some connection to their life.

That's just what synchronicity is . . . a series of coincidental events.

But sometimes signs don't come with bells and whistles. There is no fanfare, no dramatic event that flashes like a neon billboard shouting, "Pay attention! This is a sign!" No, sometimes a sign can be as subtle as a feeling in the pit of your stomach. I'm sure you've felt it before. It's that little niggling feeling that something isn't quite right, or a little voice inside of you that tells you to pay attention and be careful.

For example, let's say you're looking for a new home and spend an entire day going in and out of open houses. You find something wrong with every house you see, but then you come across one that has everything you want: it's the right size, the right style, in the right neighborhood, and the right price. It even has the kind of backyard you've always dreamed of. Yet for some reason, you have a feeling that this isn't the house for you. You can't put your finger on a specific reason, but you just know that something is not right. My advice to you would be to trust your instincts. You could be getting a prediction of problems that will occur in the house if and when you move in. It could be a boiler that breaks down or a roof that needs repair or a basement that will flood the first time you have a heavy rain. Your guides could be giving you a heads-up on a problem that may come in the future.

I know some of you may be thinking that it would be silly to pass up a dream house just because of a feeling, that there could be other factors making you feel off. That's true, and that's why you have to question why you feel the way you do. Is it the ugly paint color on the walls and the shag carpeting from the '70s that turn you off? Certainly not good reasons not to buy an otherwise perfect house. But in order to find out if the feeling you're getting is an actual sign or if you just have agita over someone's bad decorating taste, I recommend you visualize the house as you would decorate it. Walk around imagining the colors you'd paint the walls; picture your own furniture in the rooms. If you still have a bad feeling after this visualization exercise, go with your first instinct and pass on the house.

There could be one other reason you have a negative feeling about the house—you're picking up the energy of the people who previously lived there. Maybe the former owners fought a lot and eventually got a divorce. You may be picking up the residual negative energy of their disagreements. Ask your real estate agent about the owners and see what you learn. That said, this certainly isn't a reason not to buy the house. If we all refused to buy homes because the previous owners fought or divorced, there wouldn't be any sellable houses on the market. If the house is perfect in every other way, you should seriously consider purchasing it. I would suggest you just clear out that negative energy as soon as you move in. (In fact, I recommend you do this whenever you move into a new place; you never know what went on in the home before you got there.) It's quite simple to do: in a spray bottle you can buy at the drugstore, make a mixture of a half teaspoon of sea salt or kosher salt and about six ounces of lukewarm water (warm enough to dissolve the salt). Starting with the outside of the house, just spray the salted water all along the perimeter of the home. Then go inside and lightly spray every room, starting in the corners and working your way to the center of each room. Try not to spray the walls or the floor; you just want to cleanse the atmosphere. Next, try smudging the atmosphere by burning a smudge stick. (Smudging is a cleansing technique usually involving smoke). To make a smudge stick, tie together a variety of different dried herbs such as lavender, sage, or mugwort. I recommend obtaining the ingredients via the Internet, but you don't necessarily need all the ingredients to cleanse your home. You can just go to your neighborhood grocery store and buy a bottle of dried sage. Then put a tablespoon of sage in an ashtray and burn it. (If you can't find sage either, don't worry—the salt water should do the trick.) You don't have to keep the sage burning for hours (it smells pretty bad); just walk about the rooms with the sage burning for a few seconds and you're done. Since I'm Catholic, I always top the routine off with a sprinkle of holy water for an extra blessing.

The bottom line is you should pay attention to your feelings; you never know when they could save you from making a very costly mistake.

Sometimes you may get some resistance if you try to follow your signs because others may not see or feel what you're sensing. Your spouse may think you're nuts for refusing to buy what appears to be your dream home all because of a feeling, but stand by your convictions. Let people think you're crazy or just being stubborn. They might not understand you, but your guides won't lead you astray. I know how hard it is. There are times I still get angst when others think a decision I make is illogical. But once I get a bad taste in my mouth about a situation, I just can't move forward, and I will have no regrets because I trust my guides totally.

On the flip side, there may be times you feel so magnificently optimistic about something that nothing or no one can make you feel down about it. When you feel this good, believe that things will turn out right for you, no matter how unrealistic everyone else may think you are being. Ignore the naysayers and follow the signs toward your dreams. If you don't listen to the signs and ignore the feeling in your gut, you'll be kicking yourself and always second-guessing the decisions you made.

If you can learn to trust yourself and listen to your instincts, you won't be misled. In fact, I believe your intuition is the best guide you have. I remember one time my intuition literally saved my life. It happened several years ago, after I was recovering from unsuccessful back surgery. I was in a lot of pain, and my doctor prescribed an anti-inflammatory for me. It didn't kill all the pain, but it worked well enough and didn't cause me any side effects.

Then one day, when I went in for a regular checkup, my doctor suggested a new medicine. "There's a new anti-inflammatory on the market and all the tests show it works better than anything else out there. I'm going to give you a couple of sample boxes and you can give them a try."

My stomach immediately went into a knot. I felt my blood rush to my face and my blood pressure rise. I took this as a sign that the medicine wasn't good for me. So I said to the doctor, "Thanks, but the medication I've been taking is working just fine. If you don't mind, I'd rather not start playing around with something new."

"But this medicine is better," he countered. "Give it a try and you'll see."

All of a sudden, I felt rage build up inside of me. I don't know why. True, I had sensitivities to certain medications, so it's understandable that my internal alarms would react to a new prescription, but the loathing I was feeling for the doctor at that moment seemed quite extreme. I knew he believed he was giving me something better, but nevertheless, I was still feeling angry.

My feelings weren't making sense, but I'd learned to trust myself, so I said, "Listen, Doc, I know you mean well and I appreciate your thoughtfulness, but I come from the old school that says, If it ain't broke, don't fix it. So let's just keep me on the old meds and I'll be fine."

I could see by the look on his face that he didn't want me to win this battle. "I understand your concerns, Mary, and I'll make a note of them. But I don't foresee you having any problems with these pills." He handed me six boxes of the samples. "I'll tell you what," he continued, now trying to bargain with me, "you take these for a few days and if they bother you, just call my office and I'll call your old prescription in to the pharmacy."

"No!" I screamed at him. "You may not foresee a problem, but I do and I don't want to take them!"

I couldn't believe I was having an argument with my doctor. I was so shocked by my behavior that I took the samples of the medication and left the office, telling the doctor I'd give it a try and call him if there were any problems.

Don't think I was ignoring my instincts. I had no intention of taking those pills. I would just call my doctor in three days and say the new anti-inflammatory didn't agree with me and have him call in my old prescription. I still had enough of my old medication to last a few days, and when it comes to my health and well-being, I'm not above telling a little white lie. I usually don't like to lie at all, but I was sure this medication would be bad for me, so I had no other choice.

So, as planned, three days later I called the doctor's office and spoke with his medical assistant. She was aware of my agreement with the doctor, and when I told her the new medication made me ill, she said she'd give the doctor the message and make sure he called in my old prescription. The next day, I called the pharmacy to see if the doctor had done as he promised, and he had. That more or less ended the story. I did, however, eventually switch doctors and had no further problems getting my prescription.

Then one evening, my daughter Jackie and I were having dinner and watching the local news. All of a sudden, the hairs on my arms stood on end as I heard the reporter mention the name of the medication that doctor had wanted me to take. The report said that there seemed to be a problem with the new anti-inflammatory. There were at least two reported deaths connected with this medication, and countless other patients who reported major liver problems. Apparently, the problem wasn't with the drug itself, but with the way doctors had been prescribing it. This new drug was never intended to be used for chronic pain or for extended use. The reporter ended his story by telling viewers that if they took the medication they should see their doctor immediately and be tested for liver malfunction.

Two weeks later, I received a call from the office of the doctor who had wanted me to take the anti-inflammatory. The medical assistant who called told me I needed to come in and have my blood tested for liver problems. I told her that I was familiar with the report about the adverse effects of the medication, but I wouldn't need testing. I confessed that I had fibbed and never took a single pill. Needless to say, she was left speechless, but I didn't care. I was just grateful that I had listened to my intuition and fought for what I knew was right for me.

I hope this story will teach you that you don't have to be a professional psychic to have predictions. We all have gut feelings and we should listen to those signs. Your instincts will help you make the call on what's good for you or not. And don't worry about upsetting a few people along the way. The only person you have to please when it comes to your well-being is yourself.

Your intuition won't let you down, I promise you. Just learn to trust yourself, and you won't go wrong. I do want to share with you, however, that at times you may not see immediate validation of your instinct. Sometimes predictions take U-turns. But just because there are some twists and turns doesn't mean that a certain prediction won't come to pass. It only means it won't happen as quickly as you anticipated. Don't let this delay make you second-guess yourself. Have faith in your intuition and wait to see what happens.

Even after being a professional psychic for more than twenty-five years, some of my predictions take a while to be fulfilled. I'll admit that I may have a moment or two of self-doubt, but in the end I always trust myself—and I haven't been disappointed yet! I remember one time my intuition was very strong but what I predicted seemed as if it weren't going to happen, so much so that I began to think it didn't just take a U-turn, it took a wrong turn and kept on going! But seriously, it did take a little longer than I had expected but it finally came to pass.

It was late 2003 and my first book, *Beyond These Four Walls*, was coming out in February 2004. Heather, my publicist from Berkley, and I were discussing which shows we should pitch in hopes that I would get some national media to kick off my book tour. Heather went through the usual options and then when she said *The Wayne Brady Show*, a chill went up my spine.

"That's it, Heather! I'm going to be on *The Wayne Brady Show*!" I exclaimed.

Heather chuckled and told me she was glad I was so confident, but warned me not to get my hopes up too high. Getting booked on a national television show isn't that easy. There is a lot of competition and only a small number of authors get on. But I told her that my gut instinct was telling me that I'd be on Wayne Brady's show—I was sure of it.

A few months later, in November 2003, I was scheduled to be in Los Angeles to appear on a local morning news show. Heather called me a few days before I was to leave and told me there was a possibility that I would be able to meet a producer from *The Wayne Brady Show* and give her a reading. Now I didn't just get a chill up my spine, the hairs on the back of my neck stood up! "This is it!" I thought. I was going to meet someone from Wayne's show and then for sure I would be booked. I knew it as sure as I knew my own name.

I arrived in L.A. a few days before I was to be on the morning show. I was to connect with the show's producer and figure out a time that we could meet. But somehow, our schedules didn't work and I wound up giving her a reading over the phone. Needless to say, I was disappointed. I could have given her a phone reading from New York, and I felt sure I had to meet someone from the show *in person* before I would be booked. Was my intuition off? Would I even get on the show? My confidence was shaken and I allowed myself a few moments of uncertainty. But then I recalled what a strong feeling I had had when Heather first mentioned *The Wayne Brady Show* and I knew it would happen. I just had to surrender this to the Universe. I had done all that I could and now it was out of my hands.

I had to be grateful to the Universe for allowing me the privilege of appearing on any television show, even if it wasn't national. Hell, I was lucky to be in California at all, considering that it wasn't so long ago that I could barely get out of my bed because of my illness. I knew I was truly blessed, and reminded myself that listening to my instincts had gotten me as far as I had come. They helped me pursue my dream of having my book published; they enabled me to accept the invitation to start doing seminars; and they allowed me to find the medication that eventually allowed me to move beyond the four walls of my home. All huge miracles, as far as I was concerned.

The following morning I got up bright and early, excited to be appearing on the morning news show. I admit, I had a few butterflies floating around in my tummy, but I didn't let them get the best of me. There was no way I was going to allow my own insecurities to rob me of enjoying my experience on television. I remembered the signs and synchronous events that had led me there and I had surrendered the outcome. So why should I be nervous if I truly believed I was being looked after by a higher power?

As I waited in the greenroom until I was called to appear on the set, I noticed a white sheet of paper on a table. My instincts told me to walk over and take a look, so I did. At the top of the paper was the date and then a list of the guests that were to appear on the show that day. I perused the list excitedly, anticipating reading my own name, when my eyes locked on the first guest to appear. "This can't be," I said to myself. I looked down at the paper again and I still couldn't believe my eyes. I turned to John, my media escort who had driven me to the show that morning. "John, get a load of this," I said as I handed him the paper.

"Wayne Brady? Weren't you just talking about him on the way over here?" he asked.

I had mentioned to John that I hoped to meet someone from Wayne's show on this trip, but it hadn't worked out.

"Wayne Brady is appearing on the same show as I am. Can you believe it?" I asked. "The odds are too incredible for this to be just a coincidence."

"What do you think it means?" John asked, perplexed and a little amazed.

"I really don't know yet, but I'm sure we'll soon find out."

My heart was pounding a mile a minute because I knew this was a sign . . . a huge freaking sign. I knew that there were no such things as coincidences and everything happens for a reason, so I tried to make sense of what was going on. I thought about all the synchronous events that had led up to this moment:

1 ✦ My publicist Heather and I discuss pitching *The Wayne Brady Show* and a chill runs down my spine—a sign to me that I would be appearing on the show.

2 ♦ Heather tells me she has arranged for me to connect with a producer from the show and I get a second premonition that leads me to believe that I will actually meet someone from the show and then get booked to appear on the show.

3 ♦ I don't get to meet the producer in person and question if I will actually get on the show. I'm extremely disappointed but surrender the outcome to the Universe.

4 ♦ Wayne Brady just happens to be appearing on the same local television show as I am, on the same day, within ten minutes of each other.

I wasn't sure how this was all going to play out, but I knew it was out of my hands. I would be fine whatever the outcome because I was, no doubt, in the presence of divine intervention.

Wayne was scheduled to go on before me, but at the last minute a producer ran over to me saying Wayne was running late and I was to go on in his place. I was rushed to the set and hooked up with a microphone when we all heard footsteps running down the hall and a man shouting, "I'm here! I'm here!"

It was none other than Wayne Brady. Everyone on the set smiled when they saw him. I quickly got up from the chair where I was sitting and made room for Wayne. We exchanged a quick hello and a handshake, and he sat down with only seconds remaining before he was live on the air.

I sat on the sidelines watching him and waiting for my turn to go on after he was through. I couldn't believe I was seeing Wayne Brady in the flesh. What a rush!

Wayne finished up his interview and formally introduced himself to me as I went to take his place on set. Even though we spoke for the briefest of moments, he was very nice and friendly, and then he took off.

My five-minute segment went smoothly. The cohosts interviewed me, asking about my psychic ability and my upcoming book, and I gave them both quick on-air readings providing as much information as I could in such a short time. I must say I wasn't very pleased with how the readings turned out. There was just too little time to connect and I didn't feel blown away by the information I was receiving. I was disappointed, and I couldn't understand why my guides would have me come all this way—three thousand miles from home—to do mediocre readings on television. I was puzzled, but not depressed. It was what it was. I just had to surrender it.

After my segment was done, I stayed around the studio a little while longer giving readings to a few people I had promised earlier. The first person I'd promised to read met me in the greenroom. She was a lovely woman with clear and positive energy, yet I didn't feel connected with her. I tried and tried, but I felt like a kid with ADD. I felt like I had ants in my pants and just wanted to get out of there. But I had promised her a reading, and I was going to try my best.

As I concentrated, a grandmother who had passed over came through, telling me that she and her family were from Florida. I conveyed the message to the woman but this made no sense to her. I tried again and received other names of people who had passed over, but she said the names meant nothing to her. I was stumped. The information was coming in loud and clear but it didn't seem to be for this woman. Energies sometimes get intertwined, but that usually only happens at seminars when there are a lot of other people around. There was no one in the greenroom except me and this woman.

I was stuck on this grandmother from Florida and finally had to apologize to the woman. I told her I just wasn't getting any help from the Other Side and I didn't think the reading would work today. She left, disappointed, and the next person I promised to read came in.

For whatever reason, this reading was going much better than the first. I was getting a lot of information from this person's loved ones. And just when it seemed like I was totally released from my Florida grandmother, I began seeing Wayne Brady in my head. I tried to get him out of my head. I was probably thinking about him because I just met him. I tried to concentrate on the person sitting in front of me and continue with the reading, but Wayne popped back in my head, and this time he was with the grandmother from Florida. I was getting frustrated, and told the woman I was reading what the problem was.

"Oh, maybe you're picking up Wayne's energy because he's still here," she ventured.

"What do you mean he's still here? Didn't he leave as soon as his segment was done?"

"No, I was just talking with him right before I came in for my reading with you. I bet he's still in the parking lot hanging out."

Immediately, I knew why I was having so much trouble with the readings. My guides were trying to tell me to get my butt outside. They were showing me signs of Wayne's family (I had forgotten he was from Florida) and I just kept dismissing them. Now I knew what I had to do. I excused myself from the reading and ran out to the parking lot.

As I opened the studio doors in a panic, I spotted my media escort John waiting by the car.

"John, have you seen Wayne Brady?" I asked frantically. I hoped I hadn't missed him.

"Yeah, he's right there," John responded, pointing to my right about fifteen feet away.

I had my shot and I took it. "Wayne, hold up! Can I have a minute?" I yelled.

Wayne looked up and smiled and said, "Hey, Mary! What's up?"

I was shocked that he remembered my name, but quickly got over it because I knew that this was my one chance to get on his show. I quickly explained that I was having trouble doing readings inside because I was stuck on him. I relayed the messages I was getting and they all made sense to him. Then I told him that I'd just read a producer from his show the previous day in an attempt to get on his show when my book came out.

"Great! When are you going to be on?" he asked.

When I told him it was still up in the air, he asked for my business card, promising that he'd have someone get in touch with me to set something up.

I couldn't believe this was happening. I started digging frantically through my bag to find a card for him. I soon got frustrated and knelt on the ground to empty my big bag of its contents so I could find a business card. Out came my homemade bread, which I carry around in a plastic bag wherever I go. I pulled out the purple insulated bag that keeps my medication cool. Then out came two bottles of spring water and some tissues . . . but still no business card. I could feel Wayne staring down at me. He must have thought I was homeless, carrying all my possessions around with me. I was embarrassed and quickly explained that I had to carry all this stuff because I had multiple sclerosis. I told him I had to keep my medication chilled, and I carried the water because that's all I could drink and the homemade bread because I couldn't eat in restaurants.

Wayne couldn't believe I had MS because I was so full of energy and pep. I told him I had written a book about my life and my struggle with the illness and that I wasn't always so energetic. That I, in fact, had been homebound for many years, disabled by the disease. I credited my medicine, Prokarin, and a strict diet with getting me as healthy as I was. Wayne was obviously impressed. "I love your energy," he said. "You've got to come on my show!"

And that's the miracle U-turn I received to get on *The Wayne Brady Show*. I had received all the signs, but for a while there it didn't seem like it was going to happen. I could have gotten depressed when it looked like my signs weren't panning out. I could have whined and complained because things didn't look like they were working out. But I trusted my instincts and surrendered the outcome to the Universe. And by going with the flow and keeping myself open to the possibilities, my premonition eventually came true.

Remember that sometimes your premonitions may seem illogical or totally off the course, but even when things look like they won't happen, an unexpected U-turn can make your dreams come true. All you have to do is clear your energy path and recognize the signs the Universe is sending you when you're in need. When in doubt, keep that in mind and never forget that the best guide you have is you!

12.

Not Another Frog

How to Choose the Right Life Partner

The minute I heard my first love story,
I started looking for you, not knowing how blind that was.
Lovers don't finally meet somewhere
They're in each other all along.

—Rumi

You may be asking yourself, "What does a psychic medium who speaks to the dead know about love and romance?" Well, let me begin by saying that I'm a human being just like the rest of you who's had her share of romance, both good and bad. And let me also add that before I became a psychic medium, one who speaks to those beyond, I was a psychic intuitive whose main readings were for people who were looking for love or wanted help with their ongoing relationships. Oh, there were also those who came to me for life direction, but a very high percentage of my clients came—and continue to come—to me with the hope that I'll be able to guide them to the right mate, or what they commonly refer to as their soul mate. They all want to find "the one," and express frustration about not meeting the person who is their "other half." (Although throughout this chapter I will be referring to your soul mate as "the one," I don't want you to think we only have one soul mate in our lifetime. That's simply not true. I've known many people lucky enough to find a soul mate and spend many wonderful years together until death parts them, and then go on and find another soul mate. Also, soul mates are not necessarily all romantic partners. I'll explain more about that later.)

For some, finding a soul mate feels as confusing as trying to put together a 10,000-piece jigsaw puzzle without having a picture to guide them. Yet, for others it's as easy as eating a piece of cake. Why? Well, there isn't one simple answer, but then again it's really not all that complicated either. I believe the ease or difficulty of a person's love life is solely determined by whatever life journey they're on and the lessons their soul has chosen to learn this time around. Yes, you heard me right . . . I said *chosen*.

I know that to those of you who have had disastrous relationships in the past, the concept that you chose the path you're on is mind-boggling, especially if your heart has been broken time and time again. But it's true, at least to some extent. You see, according to the laws of evolution and reincarnation, we choose the battles we fight and the hurts we go through in each life. Our actions in a past life cause us to be placed in an environment in this life that can best help develop whatever traits we are lacking or learn any lessons we need to learn. Evolution is like the army; it helps you be all that you can be!

I'm sure most of you have heard of the reincarnation theory, the concept that we've all lived before. And although most of the general population seems to be aware of the theory, I realize by the questions I'm asked that not everyone understands it. So I've taken the liberty of answering some of the questions you may have.

Q • *What does it mean to be reincarnated?*

A ♦ Reincarnation is the rebirth or the transmigration of the soul from one body to another. Some would say it's the soul's journey between the physical domain and the spiritual domain.

Q ♦ *Does the soul ever die?*

A ♦ No, the soul continues to live after the termination of the body. But it rests in between incarnations in a place that some call heaven. Others may just say that the soul rests in complete peace surrounded by feelings of love.

Q ♦ *If our soul goes to heaven, then why does it choose to come back here and do it all over again?*

A ♦ When the soul reaches heaven, it studies the life it has just completed and then judges how successful it was in fulfilling the task it laid out for itself its last time on earth. When the soul sees how well, or how not so well, it has done, it then decides what it needs to try to accomplish next time around.

Q ♦ *When does a soul decide to return to another body?*

A ♦ The soul returns when it feels that a certain person or family can help it accomplish the spiritual goals that it didn't achieve, or was lacking in, last time around.

Q ♦ *Is the process of reincarnation a punishment, like what the Catholic religion refers to as purgatory or hell?*

A ♦ Western religion calls our mistakes "sins," and therefore one may believe that coming back to earth after death is a punishment for any imperfections or wrongdoing. Eastern religion calls it "karma" (what goes around comes around). Karma and sin make us feel like we have to *pay* for our mistakes, but the soul wants to be as perfect as it can be so it can stay in heaven with God, or the higher power, forever. So, if going back to earth is a punishment, it's a self-inflicted one because the soul decides and judges for itself when, where, how, and with whom it will come back. The only reason the soul wants to come back here at all is to complete its spiritual journey so maybe someday it won't have to pack its spiritual luggage one more time and do it all over again.

Q ◆ *Do past lives determine what we'll be or do in this lifetime?*
A ◆ No, past lives only *influence* this lifetime. How far we go once we get here is all our own doing. But we do get a lot of help from our angels and guides through so-called coincidences and signs.

That last point is something I really want to emphasize. Although we choose the lessons we believe our soul needs to learn before we are ever conceived, and that determines who and what we'll be in this lifetime, it is up to us to learn those lessons in the years, or even the hours or minutes, that we are here on this plane. And just as we're graded in school, we will eventually be graded on how well we performed in the school of life. But the one who does the judging is the soul itself. It determines what more it needs to learn and decides to come back when it believes a certain lifetime can help it become more perfect.

When the soul is done with this lifetime, it leaves the body. On its journey to heaven, it is greeted by its angels, guides, old friends, and family members who have passed on. The soul acknowledges its cheering entourage and then goes through a life evaluation by viewing an instant replay of the life it has just left. You've heard people say when they were moments away from death due to an accident or other life-threatening situation that "their life flashed before their eyes." Well, that actually happens once we cross over. Everything flashes before our eyes. All the good we've done, as well as all the mistakes we've made, becomes very clear to us. Honestly, it's not a film I'm looking forward to seeing anytime soon—at least not without some editing before I go. But the great part of it is that we are capable of editing while we're here. As long as there is a breath in our bodies, we can fix our imperfections and make this life journey better.

Our soul continues to learn as long as we are alive. We can be as old as the oldest person in history, confined to a wheelchair and breathing with the help of a respirator, and still be able to edit our past mistakes.

Think of your entire life as a classroom and God or the Universe (whichever you prefer to call the higher power) as your professor. And the signs we receive are our flash cards, helping us to do the right thing to help us stay on track. Once you understand that your purpose here is to learn, the simpler it will be for you to find your way in this life.

So, what does all of this have to do with finding true love? A couple of things, actually.

Over the years, I've learned that everyone's love path is different. I've met couples who had the easiest time meeting each other. They said they felt their meeting was predestined because they had experienced a déjà vu feeling upon their first encounter—a feeling they had met each other at another time, another place.

Other couples, who have had disastrous relationships in the past, said they never thought meeting the love of their life would be easy because of their bad track record in affairs of the heart. But, they added, they were pleasantly surprised by just how easy it was once they met the right person. Most felt their meetings were divinely inspired because everything leading up to their first embrace was just one synchronistic coincidence after another. Why did they find it so easy this time around? In one word: timing!

Sometimes, in order for us to find true love, some of us have to go through major trials and tribulations. Why? Because it's not just your soul that has to be ready for love, your soul mate has to be ready for you too! Both of your karmic paths have to be cleared for each other.

I know what you're thinking. What about all those times we felt so sure we'd met the right person, our one and only, the love of our life, 'til death do us part, soul mate, only to be devastated by heartbreak in the end? I've asked myself the same question and finally figured out it's all because of reincarnation. You see, you may have felt all those things others have felt when they met their true loves: you had the déjà vu feeling. You too believed your introduction was heaven-sent. But what went wrong was that you confused a romantic soul mate with someone you were just *familiar* with from a past life. What screwed you up was *that old familiar feeling*. And everything you've ever been told about love said that when you sense that feeling about a person, they must be *the one*. Well, your intuition was right: you did have a connection to that person. But that doesn't necessarily mean it was or should now be a romantic connection. What happened was you didn't realize you could get *that old feeling* about any person that you connected with in a previous life.

Don't feel bad about making a mistake in finding a romantic soul mate, because you weren't the only one in the relationship who made the error. The other person did the same thing. Both your souls felt comfortable being with each other for a time. You both felt that déjà vu feeling and most likely everything was going just terrific . . . for a while.

I bet that if you look back on your relationship honestly, you'd remember that you received signs that the relationship wasn't right. Maybe your relationship began to fizzle. You started to argue a bit more. Maybe one or both of you started to become disenchanted. Things your partner did were no longer cute—they became annoying. Or maybe it was just a nagging feeling in the pit of your stomach, a tiny voice inside that said that possibly things weren't as great as you first thought they were. But you pushed that all aside, attributed your feeling to butterflies or your jealous streak or a bad day or whatever, until reality punched you in the stomach and made you realize that the person you thought was "the one" really wasn't.

Don't beat yourself up about it. We've all done it. There's no point in worrying about the could'ves, should'ves, would'ves. Don't look at past relationships as mistakes. View them as lessons.

If the person you're currently dating, or someone you date in the future, seems familiar to you, just keep in mind that they might not be your romantic soul mate. If they begin to make you miserable, if you start feeling that something isn't right, pay attention. If you don't, you may have the same rotten relationship over and over again. And do you really want a soul that made you miserable in one lifetime to follow you here again? I didn't think so.

But I don't want you to assume the worst about every new love interest that comes your way, or analyze every new relationship to death. Relax and enjoy the journey. And if you get the feeling that things aren't right, don't automatically call it all off. Just pay attention, learn to trust yourself, and try to differentiate between your own insecurities, romantic fantasies, and the influence of others such as friends and family.

But before we go any further with our discussion regarding soul mates, let's first determine who and what a soul mate actually is. A soul mate can be a soul you met in a past life or a soul you will bump into in a future lifetime. Contrary to popular belief, soul mates are not always exclusive to romance. It is anyone you have a deep connection to, including your parents, children, even your best friends. Souls tend to travel together through lives, so people you are close to here likely were connected to you in another life. (For more information about reincarnation and soul mates, pick up Brian Weiss's excellent book, *Many Lives, Many Masters*.)

But I know the soul mate you're most concerned with is the romantic kind, and you want to know how to find him or her. Once again, it's all about intuition. I really believe people know immediately if they've found the right person for them.

So how can you tell a frog from a prince (or princess)? Easy. Just trust your first impressions. I realize that not everyone is a psychic, but I also know that everyone has some sort of psychic ability. If you're shaking your head right now saying, "Oh no, I don't," I'm telling you you're wrong. Everyone has the ability to sense what's good for them and sense what's not good for them. It's simply a matter of being aware of the signs and trusting your feelings.

Now, if you're still not convinced you can spot the signs, let's start logically. Finding a romantic soul mate can feel like putting together an enormous jigsaw puzzle without any picture to guide you. Those of you who are familiar with putting together puzzles know that it's usually easiest to first put together the frame of the puzzle. It's the same with looking for love. Start with the framework, and by this I mean start with the basic criteria of what you need and want in a mate. Make a checklist of your likes and dislikes. Think about what's acceptable and unacceptable to you. And I don't mean the superficial stuff. It's not about what car he drives or what color hair she has. I'm talking big picture. If someone calls you every night, do you think that person is being attentive and caring, or do you think the person is overbearing and smothering you? Do you think someone who is extremely driven by his or her career is ambitious and focused or a workaholic who is no fun? The first step is figuring out what *you* want and then determining how the person you're with fits into that image.

But beware, because the checklist method, although logical, isn't foolproof. After all, love isn't logical. Sometimes a person can have all the attributes you're seeking and still things don't turn out right. There may be no chemistry, no connection. And I've met plenty of men and women who are deliriously happy and in love and say that their mate is nothing like what they thought they wanted.

So, what do you do? Learn to recognize the signs and feelings you get. And if you're still convinced you're not getting signs, then ask for them. For instance, let's say you're dating a guy named Anthony and you aren't sure what's going on with him. Maybe you haven't heard from him in a while. You might say aloud or even think something like: "Dear guardian angels, can you help me out here and show me what's up with Anthony?"

Now don't expect Anthony to knock on the door or call on the phone as soon as you utter those words. Could it happen? Sure, but it's better to just be aware and see what happens. You could be thinking about Anthony and "your song" comes on the radio. A good sign. Or you might unexpectedly hear from an old boyfriend the next day. That could be the Universe's way of telling you to look elsewhere. Maybe Anthony will call and tell you he had to go out of town suddenly on an impromptu business trip. Or the call could be from one of your girlfriends telling you she spotted Anthony out with another woman. It might not be the sign you want, but signs always tell the truth.

Of course, you should also ask yourself some questions and see what kinds of feelings they evoke. For instance, if you ask yourself if you can see yourself spending the rest of your life with this person, does your heart feel light or do you get a queasy feeling in the pit of your stomach? When you think about spending time to-gether, do you get excited or do you get nervous and jumpy? Re-member, when you're with the right person, you're supposed to feel good. I can't tell you how many times I hear clients talk about their relationships and tell me that when they are getting ready for a date their hands get clammy or they feel nauseous . . . and they think this is a sign of love! I don't know about you, but when I think of being in love, I don't think of throwing up. True love doesn't make us cry, it doesn't confuse us, it doesn't make us ill. True love makes us feel good. It makes us feel whole. To take a cue from the movie *Jerry Maguire*, love completes you.

I'm sure you know someone whose relationship was so full of drama, it rivaled the best story lines on the daytime soaps. People in relationships like this don't need psychic guidance; they need the help of a good therapist, a moving company, and a divorce lawyer! Their relationship is so obviously bad everyone can see it . . . except them.

But I'm not here to make light of people who are blinded by love. Hey, we've all been there before. Many of us fail to see the signs of a bad romance because we become lost in the fantasy of love. We create our own reality where our mate and our relation-ship are perfect. We get so caught up in our own creation, we fail to see the truth that's right in front of us. We become oblivious to the telltale signs that shout out, "This person is wrong for you!"

Our first mistake is ignoring our instinct that tells us that the person we've just been introduced to, or the person we've just started dating, is a frog. Maybe we don't trust our own judgment because we think our intuition can be wrong. Well, here's a news flash: your first instincts are *always* correct. Trust them. Sometimes we unconsciously overlook the signals we receive from our guides that shout, "Pond dweller!" Or we purposely ignore them because we think we can change the frog into royalty. But keep in mind, if it looks like a frog, smells like a frog, sounds like a frog, then it must be a frog!

The person you're with doesn't just wake up one day and turn into a frog. He or she has always been a frog. You just haven't recognized it before. If you think back on a failed relationship, I'm sure you can recall the very first time your instincts told you there could be trouble brewing in paradise. Was it the first time he made an excuse to cancel your Saturday night date? Or maybe it was the time you called her house and some guy answered. I'm not saying anyone who has to cancel a date or has someone of the opposite sex answer the phone is a frog. But your instincts can always tell you when an excuse is legitimate or just a bunch of bull, or when the person who answers the phone is just a friend or something more. Ask yourself these questions. You'll get the answers.

Many of my clients—sadly, most of them women—tell me that they are hesitant to listen to their instincts because they don't trust themselves to differentiate between an actual sign and their own insecurity. They wonder if he really is acting strange or if it's their own insecurity creating a problem that isn't there. Is he being less attentive or are they just feeling needy?

I can understand where they're coming from. We're all insecure about something at some point in our lives. We all have fears or scars from old relationships that cause us to second-guess ourselves in new relationships. And you can't just wipe these insecurities away overnight. But you can take steps forward to become more sure of yourself. The best way to start is to try to determine what you want and need out of a relationship. This is a nonnegotiable list of qualities you want in a relationship: respect, trust, honesty, someone who wants to be with you as much as you want to be with them, etc. And when you feel that those needs are not being met, you have to realize that you deserve better than you're getting. You need to speak up and see if the other person changes or tell that person to hit the road.

In fact, anytime you're feeling that something is not right in your relationship, you have to speak up. If you can't tell if it is your instincts or your insecurities making you uneasy, voice your concerns to your partner. Try not to sound desperate or needy or jealous. Just explain that you're feeling uncomfortable about something—let's say an old girlfriend calling a little too often. Then give your partner a chance to explain. And while he or she is explaining, really pay attention. Don't just listen with your ears, but use all of your senses. Is your partner nervous, blushing, looking uncomfortable? What's the energy like? Is the conversation relaxed and playful or tense and upsetting?

Another sign to pay attention to is how your partner reacts to the question. Make sure your tone is not accusatory and, please, try not to cry. Instead, ask the question as sincerely and honestly as you can and see what kind of response you get. If your partner gets defensive or angry or accuses you of being jealous and insecure, realize that you're not dealing with a frog. You're dealing with a snake—a master manipulator who is trying to make you believe that you are the one causing the problem in the relationship. In this scenario, dump the bum, because this person is not just playing with your heart, he's playing with your mind. And you just don't need that in your life.

The best-case scenario is that your partner will recognize that you are being hurt and try to adjust his or her actions. When you make your partner aware of your needs, you give him or her a chance to get to know you better, and that can only lead to a better, happier relationship.

I suspect that some of you would rather not see the signs, because opening our eyes to our intuition can be painful. You don't really want to know that the person you think could be "the one" is actually a frog. But let me tell you, it will hurt more in the long run. If you were ever in a bad relationship before, remember how severe the pain was. Do you really want to go through that again? I know I don't. And if you have been fortunate to not have been heartbroken before, let me ask you a question. Are you really happy now? If you're even questioning if you're in a relationship with a frog, I know the answer is no. Please do yourself a favor and realize you deserve to be in a happy, mutually fulfilling and respectful relationship. You should be with someone who makes your heart sing.

I have personally found that it's better to be alone for a while than to be in a bad relationship. So go it alone until you find the right person. Use the time to enjoy your friends, learn about what you want and need, and, most important, nurture and take care of yourself. And the next time you're in a relationship, you'll be able to know what you need and recognize the signs that tell you if the person you're with is a keeper or a frog.

Here is a short reality checklist you can use the next time you meet someone or start a relationship. Ask yourself these questions:

* What are your instincts telling you?

* What was your first impression when you met this person?

* Are you compromising your feelings for him or her?

* Does the chemistry still feel right?

* Are you settling for something less?

+ Are you making him or her pay for someone else's mistakes?

+ Are you insecure or is the person you're with making you feel in-secure?

+ Are you happy?

You intuitively know the answers to all of the above questions—I promise you. Listen to your intuition and you won't be kissing frogs anymore!

13.

Taking Center Stage

How to Find the Job of Your Dreams

I can't tell you how many people call me complaining about how miserable they are at their jobs. I've calculated that in the past twenty-five years that I've been giving professional readings, approximately 60 percent of my clients have at one time or another been dissatisfied with their jobs. More than half of those people—more than 30 percent of my clients—say they dread getting up in the morning and going to work. Can you imagine? Thirty percent! When I think of how many people that actually comes to, it blows my mind. It makes me so sad thinking of all the wasted days people spend dreading what lies ahead for them, instead of appreciating the blessings they have.

When I express my dismay that these people have to spend half, if not more, of their waking hours being someplace and doing something that makes them miserable, I usually get the same defensive response: "What am I supposed to do? I can't help it if my boss is a jerk!" or "It's not my fault if I'm in a dead-end job."

Well, it's not your fault if you've only been at a job you despise for a week, a month, or even a year. However, it is your fault if you're schlepping to the same miserable job year after year, complaining that you hate it, but doing nothing to make a change. If you want things to get better, stop complaining and do something! I'm not saying you have to leave your job—although that might be the best thing for you. But ask yourself some questions: Do I really want to continue to feel anxious every morning before work? Is a stinking paycheck worth the aggravation, frustration, and unhappiness I feel every day? Does this job complete me? Is it what I'm supposed to be doing with my life? If you answer no to any of these questions, don't you think you deserve to put yourself on a better life path?

Look, life is not a dress rehearsal. You don't have time to be miserable. And when you complain about your job and don't do anything about it, you're putting your career energy on hold. You'll just stay stuck in the hellhole you call a job, and nothing will change or get better until you do something to recharge the energy around you. Granted, there will be times when no matter how much you enjoy your job, you just won't want to go to work. And there will be times when you will wish you didn't have to work at all! We all wish we could win the lottery and have someone feed us grapes for the rest of our lives. But that's not what I'm talking about. The vast majority of us have to work for a living. And no job should make you physically or mentally ill.

Believe me, you'll know if you're truly miserable. You've probably been that way for a while. And I hate to load some more bad news on you, but I have to be honest: the first time your gut told you that job wasn't right for you, you should have been looking for the next one, or at least have started devising a game plan to try to make things better. That funny feeling you felt in your belly was a sign that you needed to make a change, and you decided to ignore it.

Now, you may be saying, "I didn't ignore it. I just didn't know what else to do. I couldn't just walk right out. I have bills to pay and a family to feed." I understand that feeling perfectly. I've been there myself . . . but not for long. Why? Because as soon as I felt that knot in my stomach, I knew it was a sign that the job or my boss just wasn't right for me, and I started to shift my energy and my intentions in another direction. I started thinking that either the situation had to change or I had to leave it. I made a promise to myself and to the Universe that I wasn't going to subject myself to misery any longer. Don't get me wrong, I didn't quit my job on the spot, or start acting nasty or negative at work. I didn't even tell anyone I was looking for a new job. But I did begin praying and sending out messages to the Universe, letting my intention of finding a new job be known. And not surprisingly, opportunities started coming my way. I also voiced my displeasure—in a very nice and respectful way—to anyone who I felt was giving off negative energy. Whether it was a coworker who constantly complained about the job, or a supervisor who made things difficult, I always tried to be open and honest and made attempts to cleanse any negativity from the atmosphere.

Another baby step you can take toward improving your professional life is simply to look through the Help Wanted section of your local newspaper. That will clue you in to the many employment opportunities that are out there. But more than that, by looking in the classifieds you're letting your intentions be known to the Universe—you're taking your career energy out of neutral and putting it in drive. And when you start the process of actually looking for new job opportunities, things will just seem to come your way. For instance, a friend or an acquaintance may suddenly call you up and say there's a position that would be just right for you in her office.

To make the situation better in the meantime (before you get your new job), make the decision that you're not going to allow your boss to speak to you or treat you in a way that is disrespectful or unprofessional. Of course, you have to maintain a certain level of respect for your supervisor—but that does not mean he or she has the right to walk all over you. You don't even have to say anything directly to your boss. If you just voice the intention to the Universe, I'll bet you'll start to see a change in the energy around you. Your supervisor will begin to act differently toward you. Why? Because he or she will have noticed that you are different. Although your boss won't be sure what the difference is, he or she will know that something about you has changed in a positive way.

In making that decision to stand up to your boss, what you've done is taken away your own victim status—you've karmically changed the professional playing field. Your new mental attitude will lift the heavy weight of gloom from your energy. Even though you may still want to leave, you'll no longer feel like a slave to your job. (Of course, if you make that decision and your boss *still* treats you terribly, take it as a sign that you need to step on the gas as far as your job search goes. Or if, God forbid, you're being harassed or abused. If that's the case, report the person you feel is doing the harassing, and start looking for another job immediately.)

It's funny . . . as parents, one of the first things we teach our children is that if they feel uncomfortable in a situation or with certain people, they should tell someone, or make the person aware of how they are feeling. Somehow when we grow up, we forget the same rules still hold true for us as adults. If you feel uncomfortable in a situation or with a person, take it as a sign you need to make a change. Always remember the advice you gave your children still holds true for you, because you too are someone's child. You too are worthy of being respected and treated properly, and being happy with your job or career.

I want to take the time to repeat those important lessons once more. To everyone who is miserable with your present job: try making the first move, even if you don't know where it might lead you. Make the decision to change the energy in your work environment. I know it may not be your fault that you're unhappy, but take back responsibility for yourself and your own happiness. We have spirit guides to help us, but it's our job as humans to try to fix what's wrong in our lives. We should never leave our happiness in someone else's hands. Remember, only *you* own your spirit or your life force. That's your gift from God and the Universe. You can share it with others, in work and in love, but only you own it. Only you are in charge of you.

At this point you may be saying, "Okay, Mary, I get that I'm supposed to take control of my own energy and career. But . . . how do I do it?"

The first step to taking back your life force is to create in your mind's eye the best life scenario you can imagine. Simply get a piece of paper and write down a list of your fantasy jobs—the jobs you've daydreamed about having. Remember what I just said about the lesson you learned as a child—the lesson about communicating your feelings? Well, take the next step and think back to what you dreamed of being when you were young. Did you always want to be a police officer or a firefighter? If so, why not apply for a job as one? I'll talk more about this in the next chapter (about finding your calling in life), but for now, believe me when I say that the fantasies you had as a child about being a police officer, doctor, lawyer, writer, actor—whatever it was—were really signs. Signs as to what would make you feel whole in life. Signs as to what direction you should take when choosing a career path.

Of course, I'm not saying your fantasy job will work out perfectly (and I'll talk more about this too in chapter 14). Let's say you always enjoyed reading as a child, but never really considered being a writer. Well, how about becoming an editor? Or maybe going into a career that has something to do with publishing, be it books, magazines, or newspapers? I don't mean to say you should settle—your childhood career sign doesn't necessarily mean you'll be happy being an administrative assistant in a publishing company. On the other hand, it could very well mean just that. Your intuitive sign merely gives you direction as to what is the best life course for you. Where you take it, and how far you take it, is entirely up to you.

So, if it's true that we get all these signs when we're children, why is the rate of job dissatisfaction so high? Because most believe their fantasy jobs are just that—fantasies. Either that, or people believe their dream careers will just be too hard to achieve. Well, part of that may be true. If anything, life has taught me that it *is* hard work to be happy and fulfilled. You might have to work some staggering hours. You might have to deal with some awful people. Hey, if it were easy, there wouldn't be so many unhappy people in the world!

But remember this: it's always worth it in the long run. The hardest part of being happy with your job is being able to visualize what you want, surrendering your desires to the Universe, and not losing sight of your goal when the going gets rough (and I guarantee you, at one time or another it will). Even now I find myself complaining to my mother at times that between all my readings, I have no time for myself. Her favorite response to me is, "Be careful what you wish for, you just might get it." And you know, she's right . . . she's always right.

I wished for my life, and I got what I asked for. Although sometimes it's difficult, I realize I wouldn't have it any other way. Why? Because once you find what makes you happy, it's no longer a nine-to-five job. It's a twenty-four-hour job; it's part of every minute, every hour of your life . . . you and the job become one and the same. Yes, it sometimes defines who you are, but only a part of who you are. Loving your job doesn't mean you'll never have time for your family or friends. It just means that when you're with your family and friends, you'll be in a better mood and enjoy them all the more!

A quick example: it's 3:20 A.M. and I'm sitting at my computer in my office, working on this chapter. Okay, I know you may be thinking, "You work for yourself—and from your home, no less. How difficult can that be?" Or "You're your own boss and you make your own hours and you can sleep all day if you choose." My answer to all of those questions . . . "Wrong!"

First of all, I have a boss. In fact, I have many, many bosses. Let's just start with my publisher, Berkley Books. I have a contract to complete this book by a certain time and it's my job to get it done, period. But if I get up in the middle of the night because I feel inspired to do so, it's not because I have nothing to do the next day, it's because I *love* what I do. I love to write and to share the information my guides are giving me. And when you love what you do, it shows in your work and in your heart. I want you all to know I've written this book not as a chore or as a job, but because I felt privileged to be carrying out one of my lifelong dream jobs of being a writer. I thank you from the bottom of my heart for being a part of my journey.

But back to the story. My other bosses are my clients. I work for you. You make the appointments, and I give you the readings. Seeing that I'm booked seven days a week for the next year or so, I don't have much free time for lounging in bed during the day because I've been up most of the night writing. Have no fear, I'm not trying to make you feel guilty. I do get my rest, because I don't get up in the middle of the night every night—just when I'm awakened by my guides to do so. I've become a very good student of my guides. I've learned to listen to my instincts and not to dismiss them. So, I wake up with pleasure, and I read my clients with love and gratitude, because being a psychic medium is who I am. I know I am very fortunate to be able to do a job I love, the job that makes me feel complete. But what I'm here to tell you is that *everyone* has the ability to find what I've found for myself: completeness.

Let's go back to you and your job—after all, that's what this chapter is about. I'm going to give you a step-by-step plan for starting to make yourself whole in the workplace. A plan to help you create the kind of days you imagine having in the office. When you wake up, begin by simply visualizing the way you'd like your day to transpire. Believe me, the image you form in your mind really will establish what kind of day you're going to have. The good news about the Universe is that, even though you may feel like you're going off to the firing squad every time you leave your house for work, you *can* change the way you feel. You can let go of your anxiety and become optimistic, and you can do it immediately. All you have to do is surrender to your guides and the Universe.

Next, visualize the moment you first walk into work and the positive atmosphere around you. Visualize your boss greeting you cheerfully and enthusiastically. Imagine that your day will be pleasant, even if it is busy. And for good measure, imagine yourself getting a promotion or a raise. As I said before, your visualization and thoughts can actually change the crummy energy in your office, and the way your boss communicates with you and others. You can truly create a better and healthier workplace and can actually get that raise.

You can even go as far as visualizing where you'd like to be working next. But remember, you still have to make the best out of your current job while you can. Don't cop an attitude with the people you're still working with or for. In other words, while you're changing your way of thinking, don't throw the baby out with the bathwater. Don't stop working or being the best you can be at the job you're still getting paid to do. If you have the attitude that you don't care anymore about your job or the people you're working for just because you want to leave, you won't find that dream job because you'll have negative karma.

Remember, in life, good always follows good. Your job shouldn't become an energy tug-of-war. Always give your best, and the best will come to you in nature's time. Always respect where you are and be grateful that you are fortunate enough to have a job, meager as it may be. And have faith that, if you keep your intuitions intact and your energy positive, you won't be working there much longer!

When you actually get to work, even if your boss is the pain in the butt he usually is, remember that you're the one who's going to act differently today. Immediately put the white light of positive energy around you. You told yourself when you woke up that today was going to be a terrific day—now believe it! You can help yourself out by repeating a little prayer I like to say: "May the white light of the Holy Spirit wrap his arms around me and protect me against any negative thoughts and feelings that may come my way." Or you could say, "May the white light of positive energy encircle and protect me throughout the day."

Either affirmation will put a Teflon-like barrier around you. The negativity that surrounds you will slide right off your energy field, never having touched you. Repeat these words in your head: "No matter what my boss does today, he or she is not going to make me hate myself or my job." And if your boss starts busting your chops from the very beginning of the day, or anytime of the day for that matter, ask him or her, "Is there something I can do for you to make you happier with my performance?" (Sounding sincere, of course, and not sarcastic.)

If you don't follow the advice I'm giving you—if you don't take charge of your own energy—sooner or later you won't just be sick of your job, you'll actually be sick! Constantly feeling helpless and being upset is a huge strain on your immune system. Remember, everything you encounter or think about during your workday affects the rest of your life in more ways than one. Take control of the environment around you. And when the time comes, don't make excuses for not leaving your job! If you're holding out until your boss leaves or a new regime comes in and makes everything better . . . well, don't hold your breath, because it may be your last one.

The key is to listen to what your guides are telling you, and to grab those chances when they come along! Don't be afraid to take a few risks. Believe me, the Universe is looking out for you. And please, don't use the excuse that there are no jobs out there to get, because that's not true. It may be true that there aren't any jobs out there exactly like the one you're doing now. But that in itself is a sign—a sign you should be looking outside of the box.

I want to make something clear: it's one thing to put your intentions out there to the Universe. But you have to be truly willing to do the extra work that will come with the new job or promotion. You may say you understand that with a better job and a raise come more responsibilities, but have you really thought it through? You'd be shocked how many people come to me and say that they want a better position and more money . . . but also to work fewer hours. My answer to them is, "Don't we all, but it won't happen in this lifetime." You get out of work what you put into it. Put in little time, little effort, expect little money and little happiness. It's not my law; that's the law of nature.

I'm not a magician, and neither are your guides. I may be able to point you in the direction of your dream, but it's up to you to go get it. There's no shortcut, no quick fix to life. I don't have any secrets that I'm not sharing. I could talk to you until I'm blue in the face, but the fact is, if you're not willing to surrender and go after your dream, it won't come true . . . period. But on the flip side, if you *do* go after that dream—if you give your best whenever you can, send your intentions out to the Universe, and then seize the opportunity when it comes along—I promise you'll achieve your dream career.

14.

Why Are We Here?

Finding Our Purpose in Life

Whether I'm giving a lecture or seminar or I'm just on the phone with a client, nine times out of ten one of the last questions I'm asked is, "Can you tell me what my main purpose in life is?" or "Why am I here?" People want to know what they should do to give their life meaning. So, you may be asking, what does this have to do with receiving signs? Everything.

Before I begin, I just want to say that I'm not a guru or a holy person who can tell you the meaning of life. I'm not a theologian and I'm not here to profess any kind of religion or faith. I'll leave that to religious leaders who have received that calling in life.

Calling . . . I believe I've stumbled onto the magic word that will help me write this chapter, and explain how we can find our purpose in life. I've come to understand a calling as the sign a person receives that he or she is meant to do a certain task or profession, or live a certain lifestyle. A calling is a sign as to what your main purpose in life is or should be.

Most people think of a calling as something that happens to people who are chosen to join a religious order. We think of people who are "called" as extraordinary individuals who are holy, who God calls to serve Him. I know this is what I believed as a child. I attended parochial schools and was taught by nuns, and the only time I ever heard the term "calling" was when we were learning about the lives of saints. I remember studying the story of St. Bernadette, the patron saint of Lourdes, France. Bernadette Soubirous was a visionary who received messages from the Virgin Mary. After she had her visions, she became a nun and dedicated her life to prayer and the Church, and that's what I believed a calling was: dedication to one's religion.

The only time I heard the term used at home was when I was no more than eight or nine years old. It was a typical Sunday afternoon and our extended family was over for dinner. My father mentioned to the other adults at the table that his cousin's daughter had received a calling and decided to become a nun. Her calling was so strong, he said, that she was going to leave home right after she graduated high school and join the Dominican Order. The family was hoping she could postpone her plans for a few months or even a year because her mother had just passed away, and they were concerned about her father being all alone and lonely. But when they spoke to her about their concerns, she said her pull to the Church was very strong and she knew her father would be in God's hands.

"Holy cow!" I thought. My own cousin must have spoken to Our Lady . . . just like Bernadette. The women in our family never left home unless they were getting married, and here was my cousin leaving because of a feeling she had! I thought we were going to have a saint in the family!

It wasn't until many years later that I realized that we all have callings in life. God, or the Universe, or whatever you believe to be the unseen force outside our physical world, speaks to all of us through signs and callings. Everyone's life is special, whether our calling is that of a mother, husband, nurse, bricklayer, teacher, or yes, even a psychic. We all have a life path we're meant to follow that makes us feel complete and whole. Something (or some things) that makes us think, "Yes, this is what I am meant to be doing." And we all receive signs along the way to help us discover what that path is. That's what a calling is: signs telling us what we should be doing with our lives.

Let me get something clear right now: a calling could be a job or profession, but it doesn't have to be. A calling is not about what you do to earn a living. It's not about money. It's about inner satisfaction, a sense of fulfillment. You can have a calling to be a doctor, but it's not the high salary that drives you; it's the opportunity to heal people. You could have a calling to music, but that doesn't necessarily mean you aspire to perform in sold-out concerts in front of thousands. You could satisfy your calling singing in a church choir or strumming the guitar when friends come over. It's all about finding what thing in life makes you truly content deep within your soul.

Also, our calling can change with time. We can have more than one job that we love, more than one purpose in life. Take my cousin the nun for instance. She didn't stay a nun forever. Her calling lasted five years, and then she left the Church for another calling—one that said to her that she must be a wife and mother. She eventually moved to Ireland, married the love of her life, had a set of twin girls, and raised sheepdogs. Nice life, if you ask me. Just because her calling as a nun didn't last forever doesn't mean she didn't get the correct signs or that she didn't interpret them correctly for what she was supposed to do. Her calling was legitimate, she followed it, and when her next calling came, she followed that too. We can't be afraid to change if that's where we're being led. We have to be open to the signs and follow them if we expect to have a satisfying life and fulfill our purpose here.

So if we all have callings, why do so many of us have no clue what our purpose in life is supposed to be? Did we just miss the boat? I think the problem is that many people just aren't paying attention, or else they ignore the signs they are receiving because they think the calling is just too far-fetched or they believe it's too much work and they could never achieve it. They just don't have the confidence in themselves to follow the path that lies before them.

We need to become aware of the signs that are given to us, the "coincidental" events that reveal to us just what we are meant to do. Our guides will show us, and if we pay attention, we will have that "Aha!" moment when everything clicks and we realize that we're on the right track.

It happened for my daughter Jackie not too long ago. I had been asking Jackie to work for me for the past couple of years. I needed the help and knew she could do the job well. After all, she had helped me out now and then, taking phone messages and scheduling appointments, since she was twelve years old. My clients all loved her and she always did a great job. But Jackie always turned me down. She said she wanted a "real" job; she wanted to experience different things and be around different people. I didn't force the issue because I knew what she meant. She wanted to have her own journey.

Jackie said she might be interested in working as a bank teller part time while she was in school. She heard from a friend who worked at the neighborhood branch that the work wasn't too strenuous and the hours were flexible, so they wouldn't conflict with her class schedule.

I reminded Jackie that I was friendly with a few employees at the bank and told her the next time I went in I'd ask if they were hiring. And I did—I spoke with the manager, who told me that Jackie had to go to the main branch and take the teller's test, and that they would contact her when there was an opening. So Jackie went and took the test and passed. Now all she had to do was wait for them to call her. But after three weeks she hadn't heard anything and was getting anxious. School was about to start, and she wanted to have a job lined up so she wouldn't have to be worried about looking once classes started.

Again I brought up the idea of Jackie working for me. I told her I would pay more than the bank would. I assured her that this would be a real job—more than answering the phone and taking a few messages. I needed someone who would travel with me when I gave lectures or seminars, someone who could manage my business so I could focus on the readings, writing, and lectures. I had been extremely busy since the release of my book in early 2003 and it would be great if I could hire someone I didn't have to train. I told Jackie that if she didn't work for me I was going to have to hire someone else, but I would rather it was her. It would be a win-win situation for both of us. I didn't press the issue. I knew it had to be her decision. I just wanted her to know that the option was there.

About a week later, Jackie met me in the driveway as I pulled my car in. I had just gotten back from my Manhattan office, where I'd spent the weekend doing readings. I was tired after the weekend of work and the four-hour drive home. I was grateful that Jackie was there to help me in with my bags.

As soon as I stepped out of the car, Jackie asked me if the job as my assistant was still available. Surprised, I said, "Yes, why? Do you know anyone who is interested?"

Jackie smirked and said she had thought about it seriously and really wanted the job. I was delighted and I could see genuine excitement in Jackie's eyes. But what made her change her mind? I knew something had happened—I just didn't know what.

I told Jackie I was thrilled, but quite frankly a little surprised that she had made this decision. I asked her what prompted her to change her mind. Jackie smiled and said something *did* happen, and it made her feel like she was supposed to work with me. She began telling me the story that not only changed her mind, but her heart. . . .

While I was in Manhattan, Jackie was manning the phones at home, returning calls and scheduling appointments, like she usually did when I was away. It was when she returned a call from a woman named Ann that she had her revelation. Jackie asked Ann if she wanted to schedule an appointment, or if there was something else she could help her with. Ann (who I had read before) asked Jackie if she could get in touch with me because she had an emergency and needed to speak with me immediately. Jackie told her she didn't think that was possible because I was giving readings to a small group of people who had driven all the way from Philadelphia to see me. She also knew that when I gave readings I shut off my phone—including my cell phone—until I was done.

But Jackie didn't just hang up and leave this woman in a state of anxiety. She wanted to offer her some comfort and try to help her relax, so she asked Ann what was wrong. Jackie told her that maybe there was someone else she should call if this was really an emergency—like a doctor or a family member. Ann replied that it wasn't that kind of emergency. What she really needed was reassurance about an upcoming medical procedure.

My daughter used her head and told Ann that if she was leery about the procedure, she should get a second opinion. Ann said she had done that and both doctors agreed the operation was necessary, but she was still frightened about the outcome. Ann went on to say that I had given her a reading a year earlier and everything I had said came to pass, and now she just wanted to hear me say that she should have the procedure.

Jackie apologized again and said that I wouldn't be able to come to the phone for a while, but she still didn't hang up. She spoke with Ann for almost an hour, telling her she knew what it was like to be afraid of medical procedures, and that she knew firsthand how scary hospitals could be after being in the hospital herself after a major car accident.

Their conversation was coming to a close, and Jackie could sense that Ann was feeling better about the situation, but then suddenly Jackie got a feeling to try to call me on my cell phone. Even though my appointments shouldn't have been over, Jackie sensed that I was through. She told Ann she was going to put her on hold while she called me. And guess what? Yep, I had finished my readings earlier than expected and had turned my phone back on. (Yes, Jackie is a mini-me. We're connected and she can sense things and read signs, whether she likes it or not . . . although I believe she's beginning to like it.)

Jackie got in touch with me and explained what was going on, so I asked her to call me back and set it up so I could be conferenced in on the phone with her and Ann. When we were all on the line, I informed Ann that I had a very good feeling about her medical procedure and was sure her doctor would do a great job. Ann was relieved, to say the least, but I knew it wasn't me who should take credit for calming Ann's nerves. The credit went to Jackie. With conversation, compassion, and kindness, she helped Ann feel confident about her medical procedure.

Before we hung up, Ann thanked me and asked where she should send her payment. I told her I didn't want any money for answering one question. I told her I was supposed to speak with her. Together her guides, my guides, as well as Jackie's guides made sure it happened. Ann thanked me again and hung up, and that was the end of that.

Jackie said that after speaking with Ann, she really felt good inside. In her heart she knew it was a sign. She said, "When I helped Ann and saw what a difference I made in her life, it felt like the Universe had suddenly smacked me upside the head and said, 'What's wrong with you, girl? You know you're supposed to be doing this!'"

We both laughed because I knew just what she meant. And no, I don't think that meant my daughter should be a psychic medium just like her mommy. But I do believe that it means whatever job she chooses, it should be one that allows her to use her instincts, read and follow the signs, and touch and help others. With a simple phone call, Jackie found her calling and direction for her life. It was a sign she felt in her heart that let her know what she needed to do to be complete. Most of us have gotten a similar sign before, only some of us didn't pay attention or didn't realize what it was. We just have to become more aware of our feelings, and we'll be led to our destiny.

When you think of people like Oprah Winfrey, Bill Gates, or Derek Jeter of the New York Yankees, you may wonder to yourself, What drove them to become so successful? What do they have that we don't? Well, I think they had a calling to do what they are doing. They had a passion that drove them to go after their dreams and be the best they could be.

Passion . . . now there's another word that can help us understand purpose. When we find our passion in life, we have found our purpose, what we're supposed to be doing. What exactly is passion? I think of it as something that means so much to us, it's as vital as breathing. It's something we are compelled to do, and when we do it, we feel so right, so sure of who we are. One of my passions is writing. Long before I ever had a book published, long before I ever even thought that was possible, I enjoyed putting pen to paper and creating stories, or just recording my thoughts, dreams, and insights. When I write, I'm transported to another world. I can sit for hours at my computer, writing late into the night—to me that's pure pleasure. That doesn't mean that writing is not work; it doesn't mean I don't get writer's block. But the act of writing is such a joy to me, I couldn't imagine my life without it.

When you find your passion and pursue it, it shows. You're happier, fulfilled, and enthusiastic about life. I can spot a person who has found their purpose a mile away. I remember when I had the pleasure of meeting *American Idol* winner Fantasia. It was when I was on *The Wayne Brady Show*. She hadn't won yet—she was on the show with the other eleven finalists—but I knew just by looking at her that she would be the winner. In fact, I remember thinking that the first time I saw her perform on television.

I'm a huge *American Idol* fan and I never missed a show. Like the rest of America, I would watch and judge the contestants just like Paula, Randy, and Simon do. But I would also give each one a reading and try to predict how they would do in the competition. How, you may ask, can I give a person on television a reading? Well, it's the same as when I give a reading over the phone: I just try to focus in on the energy. I listen to the person's voice. And since I get to see the person on TV, I also have the opportunity to observe her body language, her aura, and—if I get a close-up—the look in her eyes. When I saw Fantasia, everything about her shouted out "Winner!" It wasn't just her singing ability that clued me in. Just watching her perform, I could see that she was doing what she loved and owned her dream. In fact, she was a winner before she even got on the show because she had found her passion.

When I met her in person backstage at Wayne Brady's show, my television reading was confirmed. As soon as I saw her, I got an image of Rocky Balboa. My guides were telling me that, just like Rocky, she was a winner against all odds. She also had a glow around her. And when I looked into her deep brown eyes, I saw that she had passion. She was already a winner. She hadn't had an easy life. Having had my first child when I was eighteen years old, I knew that Fantasia didn't have it easy raising a child when she was still a child herself. I'm sure many people discouraged her when she said she wanted to pursue a singing career. But she knew what her calling was, and she followed her dream.

Of course, I didn't tell Fantasia any of this when I met her. I just wished her good luck, as I did the other contestants. But I knew that she had passion and would become a star.

I know what some of you may be thinking. Your life is busy enough trying to do what you need to do to pay your bills, take care of your kids, and just make it through another day. Who has time to figure out what their passion is? And who has time to follow some far-fetched dream?

Please, please, please don't think like that. I can think of nothing more important than finding your purpose in life. After all, that's the reason you're here. And finding your passion is what makes this journey satisfying and worthwhile. Besides, it's easier than you might think! You just have to think back to when you were a kid. Do you remember having dreams about what you wanted to be when you grew up? Do you remember playing make-believe with wild abandon?

When we were children, we knew what made us happy. Unfortunately, though, many of us let that magic slip away. Yes, there are the lucky few who found their passions and held on to their dreams as they got older. My son Carl is a perfect example. I remember asking him when he was just seven years old what he wanted to be when he grew up. It was the day of his First Holy Communion, and he looked so handsome in his new navy blue suit. He was an intelligent kid, and he loved reading and writing. In fact, he had done so well on an essay that he had to write in preparation for making the sacrament of Communion, that the pastor of the church chose Carl to read his essay during the Communion Mass.

I was so proud as Carl read his essay, entitled "What It Means to Me to Receive the Body of Christ." Everyone was listening to his words, and I could tell many in the congregation were amazed by his writing talent and the maturity of his feelings and language. By the time he was finished, there wasn't a dry eye in the church, for every mother, father, grandparent, aunt, and uncle present was touched by the passionate way in which Carl spoke.

It was after the Mass that I asked Carl what he wanted to be when he grew up. Without a moment's hesitation, Carl answered, "I want to become a journalist." I remember looking down at him and being so proud, although I had no clue where he'd got the idea of being a journalist. It wasn't something we ever discussed at home. So I asked him if he knew what a journalist was. He answered, "Yes, someone who writes stories for a newspaper." Well, I guess he knew what he was talking about.

Carl was blessed to find his passion at seven years old and he stuck with it, no matter how many trials and tribulations came his way. And believe me, there were many times I didn't know where he got his strength to continue going to college full time while working two jobs and taking care of me and his sister. Unfortunately, as a single parent there wasn't much I could do for him financially, especially after I was diagnosed with MS. But Carl persevered, working his way through St. John's University and then graduating from Stony Brook University with a degree in communications and journalism.

I'm proud to say that at thirty years old, Carl became the editor-in-chief of a Long Island newspaper and the president of the Society of Professional Journalists of Long Island. The reason for Carl's success? He found his passion as a child and stuck with it. His passion and his determination and faith in himself enabled him to fulfill his dream.

We all can reclaim our passion. Just try to remember what you dreamed about when you were a kid. What did you love to do? What made you happy? And then try to bring that into your life today.

I can hear you now: "Mary, get real! Childhood fantasies are just that—fantasies."

I know many of you believe that your calling may be too much work, or far too hard, or too far-fetched. First, let me say that you can take baby steps toward your calling. Nothing happens overnight. A doctor doesn't receive her medical degree the first day she gets her calling. No, there are years of schooling and training that have to be completed. It's the same with anything else. You can only climb the mountain one step at a time. The most important thing to remember is that if you're following your passion, each step will be a complete pleasure.

Also, you should realize that you don't have to take your childhood fantasies quite so literally. If you dreamed of becoming an astronaut, and now you're a fifty-year-old accountant, chances are you're not going to be flying to the moon anytime soon. But that doesn't mean you can't fulfill your passion. What was it about being an astronaut that appealed to you? Were you fascinated by the planets and the stars and the vast unknown that is space? If so, you can bring that fascination back into your life. You can read books about space, buy yourself a good telescope and start stargazing, or frequent your local planetarium where they may offer classes or have a club you can join. If as a child you stood in front of a mirror singing into a hairbrush while your favorite songs played on the radio, you can recapture that love of singing by joining a church choir or getting involved in community musical theater. I said it before but I'll say it again: Your calling isn't necessarily about a job you do. It's about the essence of the job. It's not about the outcome—a paycheck, a published book, or a record deal—but about the joy you experience in the process itself. Finding your passion is all about doing what you love.

We are all here for a reason. We are all extraordinary beings with special gifts and talents. When we discover what those gifts are and use them, we can't help but be successful because we're doing what we love. If you are wondering what your purpose in life is, just think about what makes you happy, what completes you— think about what you dreamed of as a child. Those dreams are still inside you, no matter how buried they might be. Listen for your calling, watch for the signs, and your guides will lead you on the path toward your destiny.

CONCLUSION

When You Wish upon a Star

How to Make Your Dreams Come True

What lies behind us and what lies before us are tiny matters compared to what lies within us.

—Ralph Waldo Emerson

Do you remember the words to the popular Disney theme song "When You Wish upon a Star"? As a kid, I would sit in front of the television set on Sunday nights awaiting the hypnotic melody and anticipating Tinkerbell flying across the screen. And upon hearing the first note, my fantasy world would commence. I would imagine myself a character in whatever story Disney was airing that night, be it *Cinderella* or *Snow White*. I would fear the evil queen who wanted to destroy Snow White and I would feel sorry for Cinderella having to do all the chores while her stepsisters went off to the ball to meet the prince. Of course, after the show was over, I realized I was just little MaryRose who did not live in a fairy-tale world, but had to get up the following morning to go to school. And although I knew realistically that fairy tales were just make-believe, there was always some symbol or message I took from them that pertained to my everyday life.

For instance, if I couldn't go outside to play after school because I had to help my mother in the house, I would think of myself as Cinderella having to stay inside to clean. Although my mother was a far cry from the evil stepmother in Cinderella, no kid wants to stay inside to do chores or watch her little brother, and I recall that at those times, I'd wish I had a fairy godmother who could make all my wishes come true. I would imagine a rotund, happy lady tapping her magic wand and miraculously all my chores would be done. I would wish that with a click of her heels, I would become the prettiest girl in the class. I would imagine that with a snap of her fingers, I would lose all the baby fat that had been plaguing me for most of my childhood. Ah yes, if only I had a fairy godmother like Cinderella.

As I got older, I still watched Disney, but I was old enough to know the difference between fairy tales and reality. I still believed there was a real message in the song "When You Wish upon a Star." I still believed that if I wished hard enough, all my dreams would come true. And as I got older and my intuition increased as I used my psychic abilities more often, I realized that I had the power to change my life with just a thought, an intention, a desire, or a wish. And I also realized I didn't have to wish for a fairy godmother because I had one all along. I had me.

We all are our own fairy godmothers. (We do have other fairy godmothers: our angels and our guides, including our loved ones who have passed over.) We all have the power to transform our lives. Because when we wish or daydream, we're sending our heart's intentions out to the Universe, announcing our wants, and that's the first step toward making them happen. So thank you, Mr.

Walt Disney, wherever you are, for teaching us all at a very early age the first step in creating our future: wishing.

My career as a psychic intuitive has shown me over and over again that our imaginations, our dreams, and our fantasies are healthy and wonderful things and should never be stifled, ignored, or thought illogical. What may be just our fantasies today can become our reality tomorrow. I am living proof of that. For years, when I was locked behind the four walls of my home due to multiple sclerosis, I would pray, wish, hope, and dream that one day I would be well enough to drive my car again, shop in the grocery store once more, or take my grandchildren for a walk. I wished, I prayed, and at times I even bargained with God. But not until I truly understood the power of my intentions and was capable of reading the signs I was being sent, did my dreams come true. And I learned that we can all read the signs we're sent, and you don't have to be psychic to do it.

Ralph Waldo Emerson's words, "What lies behind us and what lies before us are tiny matters compared to what lies within us," seem tailor-made for this book. Although what lies behind you—the mistakes, the heartbreaks, and all—impacted your life and brought you to where you are today, your past does not define you. And no matter what you hope to accomplish, no matter how big your dreams, you can't worry about your future. The only thing you can do is focus on what you need to do right now. And the only way you'll know what you need to do is if you pay attention to the signs and listen to your intuition—that tiny voice inside of you. If you do that, your dreams will come true.

I have been given signs from my guides that have literally changed my life, and they have made me realize that we are all capable of achieving what others may think impossible. So don't let your past heartaches or setbacks stop you from dreaming about your future. And don't let someone else's definition of you stop you from believing in yourself and your dreams.

What do I mean by someone else's definition of you? Well, lots of times we allow others to label us. For instance, when I was very ill with MS I became aware that others stopped seeing me as Mary, their friend, relative, or mother of three. What I became was Mary who was sick and disabled. When I told certain people that I wanted to write a book and would one day reach thousands of people through readings and seminars, they would just smile and say, "Oh, that's nice." But what they were really thinking was, "Are you kidding? You have MS. You don't leave your house. What are you thinking?" And some people actually said that to my face.

But I ignored the negative feedback I received and dared to dream. And do you know what happened? The more I worked on making my dreams come true, the more I started believing they would. I believed I could overcome every obstacle that came my way, no matter how long it took. I believed, and the signs kept coming, and I intuitively knew what I had to do. I listened to my guides, and the more I listened, the more the signs came. In fact, what kept me afloat all the years in between my remissions was the positive signs of validation I was receiving, and the unfathomable amount of synchronous events that occurred that eventually led me to my magic kingdom of wishes and dreams. A place where I found Elaine DeLack and Prokarin, the medication that would take me beyond the four walls of my home and give me back my life. And it all happened because I followed the signs and messages I was receiving. I dared to dream and wished for a miracle, and that's what I got.

So please, always remember that the entrance to your magic kingdom, the miracle that you're praying for, lies inside your soul. All you have to do is unlock it by listening and believing the signs you receive from your angels, guides, and yes, even your fairy godmother.